Math

SPEED TESTS

REINFORCING ESSENTIAL MATH FACTS

GRADES 1—3

Written by Gunter Schymkiw

Published by
World Teachers Press®

Order Number 2-5134
ISBN 1-58324-058-6

F G H I J 08 07 06 05 04

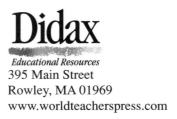

Educational Resources
395 Main Street
Rowley, MA 01969
www.worldteacherspress.com

FOREWORD ≃-+ = +-+ ≃-+ ≃-+-+ ≃-+ ≃+-+ ≃-+ = +-+-+ ≃-+ = +-+-+ ≃-+-+ ≃-+

Math Speed Tests – Book 1 provides students with opportunities to improve their rapid calculation skills with essential addition and subtraction facts.

Students enjoy the self-competition aspect of these activities while they reinforce their knowledge of essential math facts. Additional material is provided on most pages for fast finishers. This material aligns with the competency level of the speed test being done and touches areas that students find interesting.

The tests increase in difficulty and are organized with key words. For example, Test 26 is keyed to cover "+, - to 14." This test covers addition and subtraction with solutions up to fourteen. In some cases, additional review or challenge material may also be included in the test that extends beyond the overall test topic.

Titles in this series include *Math Speed Tests, Grades 1—3* and *Math Speed Tests, Grades 3—6*.

CONTENTS ≃-+ = +-+ ≃-+ ≃-+-+ ≃-+ = +-+ ≃-+ ≃-+-+ ≃-+ = +-+ +-+ ≃-+ = +-+-+ ≃-+

Test	Facts Tested	Page
	Teachers Notes	4
	Blank Master Sheets	5–6
Addition and Subtraction to 10		**7**
1	+, – less than 10	8
2	+, – less than 10	9
3	+, – less than 10	10
4	+, – less than 10	11
5	+, – to 10	12
6	+, – to 10	13
7	+, – to 10	14
8	+, – to 38	15
9	+ to 10	16
10	+, – to 10	17
Addition and Subtraction to 11		**18**
11	+ to 80	19
12	+, – to 11	20
13	+, – to 101	21
14	+, – to 83	22
15	+ to 47	23
Addition and Subtraction to 12		**24**
16	+, – to 12	25
17	+ to 107	26
18	+, – to 102	27
19	+, – to 12	28
20	+ to 12	29

Test	Facts Tested	Page
Addition and Subtraction to 13		**30**
21	+, – to 99	31
22	+, – to 13	32
23	+ to 217 and time	33
24	+, – to 13 and months	34
25	+ to 13	35
Addition and Subtraction to 14		**36**
26	+, – to 14	37
27	+, – to 157	38
28	+, – to 99	39
29	+, – to 14	40
30	+ to 68	41
Addition and Subtraction to 15		**42**
31	+ to 15	43
32	+, – to 15	44
33	+ to 15/–from 100	45
34	+, – to 103	46
35	+, – to 105	47
Addition and Subtraction to 16		**48**
36	+ to 16, 100+ and 99+	49
37	+, – to 16 and 99+	50
38	+, – to 16 and numeration	51
39	+, – to 90	52
40	+, – to 100	53
Addition and Subtraction to 17		**54**

Test	Facts Tested	Page
41	+ to 17 and money	55
42	+, – to 17	56
43	+, – to 17	57
44	+, – to 99 and money	58
45	+, – to 107	59
Addition and Subtraction to 18		**60**
46	+ to 18 and money	61
47	+, – to 93	62
48	+, – to 18 and measurement	63
49	+, – to 18 and measurement	64
50	+, – to 100	65
Addition and Subtraction to 19		**66**
51	+, – to 109	67
52	+, – to 90 and money	68
53	+ to 19	69
54	+, – to 19	70
55	+, – to 19	71
Addition and Subtraction to 20		**72**
56	+, – to 20	73
57	+, – to 79	74
58	+ to 96	75
59	+, – to 140	76
60	+, – to 20	77
Review		78
Answers		79–85

The Lesson Format – A stopwatch is needed so students can be told their times. Question types should be discussed before the students attempt each test. The tests are designed to reinforce and improve rapid calculation skills, not introduce new concepts.

Students start together. As they complete the speed test, they indicate this by calling out "finished" or putting their hands up. Tell each student the time taken and this is recorded by each student in the space provided. Activities are provided for the student to go on with when finished.

Correcting – You can use a variety of methods for correcting the tests. One approach students enjoy is saying the answers in groups of ten by individual class members.

Make a Booklet – By photocopying back-to-back, a week or term's work can be created in a small booklet. After stapling, a strip of tape can be used to keep the booklet neat.

Make Your Own – Two speed test blanks are included in this book to allow you to provide for the special needs of your students.

Individual ability levels can be met by reducing the number of problems to complete. This can be increased as students gain more confidence with their tables.

FEATURES OF MATH SPEED TESTS ⁼ ⁻ ✦ ⁼ ⁻ ✦ ⁻ ✦ ⁼ ⁻ ✦ ⁺ ⁻ ✦ ⁻ ✦ ⁼ ⁻ ✦ ⁼ ⁻ ✦ ⁼ ⁻ ✦

This page is designed to introduce and familiarize students with the tables that will be the focus of the next few pages.

Focus of this speed test.

Students complete the 50 or 100 problems on the page then indicate when finished.

Space provided for students to record their time and to evaluate their performance.

Students become familiar with the answers of the focus table.

Math Speed Tests – Book 1

1. _____
2. _____
3. _____
4. _____
5. _____
6. _____
7. _____
8. _____
9. _____
10. _____
11. _____
12. _____
13. _____
14. _____
15. _____
16. _____
17. _____

18. _____
19. _____
20. _____
21. _____
22. _____
23. _____
24. _____
25. _____
26. _____
27. _____
28. _____
29. _____
30. _____
31. _____
32. _____
33. _____
34. _____

35. _____
36. _____
37. _____
38. _____
39. _____
40. _____
41. _____
42. _____
43. _____
44. _____
45. _____
46. _____
47. _____
48. _____
49. _____
50. _____

My score: _____ My time: _____ min _____ s

The main thing I didn't understand was _____.

I now know that _____

_____.

I'm happy   I'm not happy

OOPS!   I didn't understand

1. _____
2. _____
3. _____
4. _____
5. _____
6. _____
7. _____
8. _____
9. _____
10. _____
11. _____
12. _____
13. _____
14. _____
15. _____
16. _____
17. _____
18. _____
19. _____
20. _____
21. _____
22. _____
23. _____
24. _____
25. _____

26. _____
27. _____
28. _____
29. _____
30. _____
31. _____
32. _____
33. _____
34. _____
35. _____
36. _____
37. _____
38. _____
39. _____
40. _____
41. _____
42. _____
43. _____
44. _____
45. _____
46. _____
47. _____
48. _____
49. _____
50. _____

51. _____
52. _____
53. _____
54. _____
55. _____
56. _____
57. _____
58. _____
59. _____
60. _____
61. _____
62. _____
63. _____
64. _____
65. _____
66. _____
67. _____
68. _____
69. _____
70. _____
71. _____
72. _____
73. _____
74. _____
75. _____

76. _____
77. _____
78. _____
79. _____
80. _____
81. _____
82. _____
83. _____
84. _____
85. _____
86. _____
87. _____
88. _____
89. _____
90. _____
91. _____
92. _____
93. _____
94. _____
95. _____
96. _____
97. _____
98. _____
99. _____
100. _____

My score: _____ My time: _____ min _____ s

The main thing I didn't understand was _____.

I now know that _____

_____.

I'm happy   I'm not happy

OOPS!   I didn't understand

10 + 0 = 10		5 + 5	3 + 5	6 + 3	5 + 4	4 + 2	4 + 3	7 + 0	4 + 3	3 + 0

10 + 0 = 10
 9 + 1 = 10
 8 + 2 = 10
 7 + 3 = 10
 6 + 4 = 10
 5 + 5 = 10
 4 + 6 = 10
 3 + 7 = 10
 2 + 8 = 10
 1 + 9 = 10
 0 + 10 = 10

10 − 0 = 10
10 − 1 = 9
10 − 2 = 8
10 − 3 = 7
10 − 4 = 6
10 − 5 = 5
10 − 6 = 4
10 − 7 = 3
10 − 8 = 2
10 − 9 = 1
10 − 10 = 0

5 + 5	3 + 5	6 + 3	5 + 4	4 + 2	4 + 3	7 + 0	4 + 3	3 + 0
4 + 6	5 + 2	5 + 4	1 + 8	6 + 0	2 + 1	3 + 4	0 + 3	2 + 2
3 + 7	3 + 6	4 + 5	3 + 3	4 + 5	4 + 2	1 + 2	3 + 4	1 + 5
2 + 8	5 + 3	3 + 7	4 + 6	5 + 5	2 + 0	3 + 1	1 + 5	2 + 4
1 + 9	4 + 4	2 + 8	5 + 3	6 + 4	0 + 2	4 + 0	4 + 1	4 + 2
0 + 10	2 + 5	1 + 9	7 + 2	7 + 3	8 + 2	9 + 1	10 + 0	3 + 3
10 + 0	2 + 7	0 + 10	1 + 8	3 + 6	5 + 4	4 + 4	0 + 10	1 + 4
9 + 1	8 + 1	1 + 9	2 + 8	6 + 3	0 + 4	2 + 8	9 + 1	2 + 7
8 + 2	0 + 9	9 + 0	3 + 7	4 + 5	3 + 2	3 + 7	3 + 5	6 + 2
7 + 3	6 + 4	5 + 5	4 + 6	1 + 1	2 + 3	4 + 6	5 + 5	7 + 3

Butch is very hungry. Perhaps you can help him find his way home so he can eat his dinner.

To help him you must make a path made up entirely of addition facts that equal ten. Color the path so he can see it easily.

Work neatly because Butch is a tidy dog. You can only travel up, down and across, not diagonally.

My score: _____ My time: _____ min _____ s

The main thing I didn't understand was _____.

I now know that _____

_____

1.　0 + 1 = _____

2.　3 + 2 = _____

3.　1 + 2 = _____

4.　2 + 7 = _____

5.　4 + 1 = _____

6.　1 + 6 = _____

7.　5 + 4 = _____

8.　6 + 1 = _____

9.　2 + 2 = _____

10.　3 + 5 = _____

11.　7 + 2 = _____

12.　1 + 3 = _____

13.　6 + 3 = _____

14.　4 + 2 = _____

15.　1 + 7 = _____

16.　3 + 6 = _____

17.　7 + 0 = _____

18.　5 + 3 = _____

19.　0 + 5 = _____

20.　4 + 5 = _____

21.　2 + 0 = _____

22.　6 + 2 = _____

23.　5 + 2 = _____

24.　2 + 6 = _____

25.　0 + 4 = _____

26.　4 + 3 = _____

27.　2 + 4 = _____

28.　3 + 4 = _____

29.　8 + 1 = _____

30.　3 + 3 = _____

31.　5 + 1 = _____

32.　1 + 8 = _____

33.　9 + 0 = _____

34.　1 + 5 = _____

35.　7 + 1 = _____

36.　3 + 1 = _____

37.　4 + 4 = _____

38.　2 + 5 = _____

39.　0 + 9 = _____

40.　2 + 3 = _____

41.　9 – 1 = _____

42.　4 – 1 = _____

43.　7 – 1 = _____

44.　3 – 1 = _____

45.　6 – 1 = _____

46.　5 – 1 = _____

47.　9 – 2 = _____

48.　1 – 1 = _____

49.　2 – 1 = _____

50.　8 – 1 = _____

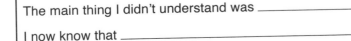

Three is a popular number in children's stories and rhymes.

Three Little Pigs

The Three Blind Mice before they met the farmer's wife.

Can you think of three more rhymes?

My score: _____　My time: _____ min _____ s

The main thing I didn't understand was _____.

I now know that _____

I'm happy　I'm not happy

OOPS!　I didn't understand

1. 7 + 2 = _____
2. 2 + 5 = _____
3. 0 + 8 = _____
4. 3 + 3 = _____
5. 5 + 4 = _____
6. 0 + 7 = _____
7. 2 + 3 = _____
8. 4 + 4 = _____
9. 3 + 6 = _____
10. 2 + 2 = _____
11. 1 + 2 = _____
12. 7 + 0 = _____
13. 0 + 6 = _____
14. 3 + 5 = _____
15. 1 + 6 = _____
16. 6 + 3 = _____
17. 3 + 4 = _____

18. 4 + 2 = _____
19. 1 + 4 = _____
20. 4 + 5 = _____
21. 5 + 3 = _____
22. 1 + 8 = _____
23. 3 + 2 = _____
24. 1 + 5 = _____
25. 4 + 1 = _____
26. 0 + 9 = _____
27. 1 + 7 = _____
28. 5 + 1 = _____
29. 2 + 6 = _____
30. 8 + 0 = _____
31. 4 + 3 = _____
32. 2 + 7 = _____
33. 2 + 4 = _____
34. 5 + 2 = _____

35. 6 + 2 = _____
36. 6 + 0 = _____
37. 6 + 1 = _____
38. 7 + 1 = _____
39. 0 + 5 = _____
40. 8 + 1 = _____
41. 6 – 2 = _____
42. 8 – 2 = _____
43. 9 – 2 = _____
44. 7 – 2 = _____
45. 3 – 2 = _____
46. 5 – 2 = _____
47. 4 – 2 = _____
48. 2 – 2 = _____
49. 4 – 3 = _____
50. 6 – 3 = _____

In mathematics "+" says:

• plus   • total

• add   • find the sum

• addition

Number Fact

A soccer team has eleven players.

How many on a baseball team? _____

My score: _____ My time: _____ min _____ s

The main thing I didn't understand was _____.

I now know that _____
_____.

1. 1 + 8 = _____

2. 1 + 6 = _____

3. 1 + 7 = _____

4. 6 + 3 = _____

5. 3 + 2 = _____

6. 3 + 5 = _____

7. 5 + 2 = _____

8. 5 + 4 = _____

9. 1 + 5 = _____

10. 7 + 1 = _____

11. 5 + 1 = _____

12. 3 + 6 = _____

13. 2 + 4 = _____

14. 9 + 0 = _____

15. 4 + 2 = _____

16. 7 + 2 = _____

17. 0 + 8 = _____

18. 5 + 3 = _____

19. 4 + 3 = _____

20. 3 + 3 = _____

21. 2 + 7 = _____

22. 6 + 1 = _____

23. 3 + 4 = _____

24. 2 + 6 = _____

25. 8 + 1 = _____

26. 6 + 2 = _____

27. 0 + 9 = _____

28. 2 + 5 = _____

29. 4 + 4 = _____

30. 3 + 6 = _____

31. 5 plus 4 = _____

32. 5 plus 2 = _____

33. 2 plus 2 = _____

34. 2 plus 7 = _____

35. 6 plus 2 = _____

36. 3 plus 3 = _____

37. 5 plus 3 = _____

38. 4 plus 4 = _____

39. 5 plus 1 = _____

40. 1 plus 1 = _____

41. 9 – 6 = _____

42. 9 – 5 = _____

43. 9 – 4 = _____

44. 9 – 3 = _____

45. 9 – 2 = _____

46. 8 – 6 = _____

47. 8 – 5 = _____

48. 8 – 4 = _____

49. 8 – 2 = _____

50. 8 – 1 = _____

In mathematics "–" says:

• minus   • subtract

• less   • take away

• find the difference

Number Fact

Insects have 6 legs. Spiders have 8 legs.
Can you think of an animal
that has 2 legs?

_____

My score: _____ My time: _____ min _____ s

The main thing I didn't understand was _____.

I now know that _____

_____.

1. 5 + 3 = _____
2. 6 + 3 = _____
3. 1 + 5 = _____
4. 1 + 7 = _____
5. 3 + 4 = _____
6. 2 + 6 = _____
7. 5 + 2 = _____
8. 3 + 2 = _____
9. 3 + 4 = _____
10. 6 + 2 = _____
11. 0 + 7 = _____
12. 1 + 7 = _____
13. 2 + 7 = _____
14. 2 + 3 = _____
15. 2 + 5 = _____
16. 8 + 1 = _____
17. 2 + 4 = _____

18. 1 + 6 = _____
19. 2 + 1 = _____
20. 4 + 5 = _____
21. 3 + 3 = _____
22. 2 + 3 = _____
23. 5 + 4 = _____
24. 1 + 3 = _____
25. 1 + 1 = _____
26. 7 + 2 = _____
27. 4 + 2 = _____
28. 3 + 6 = _____
29. 3 + 5 = _____
30. 4 + 3 = _____
31. 9 minus 1 = _____
32. 6 minus 2 = _____
33. 9 minus 2 = _____
34. 8 minus 3 = _____

35. 7 minus 1 = _____
36. 5 minus 3 = _____
37. 6 minus 1 = _____
38. 8 minus 2 = _____
39. 7 minus 2 = _____
40. 8 minus 1 = _____
41. 8 – 4 = _____
42. 8 – 6 = _____
43. 8 – 7 = _____
44. 6 – 5 = _____
45. 9 – 7 = _____
46. 5 – 3 = _____
47. 8 – 3 = _____
48. 9 – 8 = _____
49. 7 – 5 = _____
50. 6 – 4 = _____

Tip
Sometimes subtracting (taking away)
is easier if you "count up."
For example, in 10 – 9 it is easier to count on from 9 to 10
and get the answer one, than to count backwards, 9 from
10 to get the answer one.

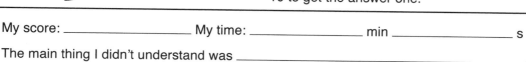

My score: _____ My time: _____ min _____ s

The main thing I didn't understand was _____.

I now know that _____
_____.

1. 6 + 3 = _____

2. 6 + 4 = _____

3. 3 + 5 = _____

4. 0 + 10 = _____

5. 7 + 2 = _____

6. 9 + 1 = _____

7. 6 + 2 = _____

8. 2 + 5 = _____

9. 8 + 1 = _____

10. 3 + 3 = _____

11. 5 + 5 = _____

12. 5 + 2 = _____

13. 3 + 7 = _____

14. 7 + 3 = _____

15. 2 + 4 = _____

16. 5 + 3 = _____

17. 1 + 9 = _____

18. 4 + 5 = _____

19. 2 + 6 = _____

20. 9 + 0 = _____

21. 2 + 8 = _____

22. 4 + 3 = _____

23. 10 + 0 = _____

24. 4 + 2 = _____

25. 3 + 7 = _____

26. 3 + 4 = _____

27. 3 + 6 = _____

28. 6 + 4 = _____

29. 4 + 6 = _____

30. 2 + 3 = _____

31. 4 + 4 = _____

32. 1 + 3 = _____

33. 8 + 2 = _____

34. 1 + 4 = _____

35. 4 + 6 = _____

36. 5 + 4 = _____

37. 7 + 3 = _____

38. 4 + 1 = _____

39. 2 + 2 = _____

40. 3 + 2 = _____

41. 9 – 3 = _____

42. 5 – 3 = _____

43. 10 – 3 = _____

44. 8 – 3 = _____

45. 4 – 3 = _____

46. 8 – 4 = _____

47. 6 – 3 = _____

48. 9 – 4 = _____

49. 7 – 4 = _____

50. 10 – 4 = _____

Measure these straight lines in centimeters.

Write their lengths in the spaces.

_____ _____ cm

_____ _____ cm

_____ _____cm

_____ _____cm

_____ _____cm

My score: _____ My time: _____ min _____ s

The main thing I didn't understand was _____.

I now know that _____

_____.

1. $1 + 9 =$ _____

2. $7 + 2 =$ _____

3. $1 + 8 =$ _____

4. $0 + 6 =$ _____

5. $4 + 6 =$ _____

6. $6 + 0 =$ _____

7. $5 + 4 =$ _____

8. $6 + 4 =$ _____

9. $1 + 5 =$ _____

10. $9 + 1 =$ _____

11. $3 + 2 =$ _____

12. $2 + 4 =$ _____

13. $0 + 7 =$ _____

14. $1 + 6 =$ _____

15. $6 + 3 =$ _____

16. $1 + 3 =$ _____

17. $2 + 8 =$ _____

18. $2 + 5 =$ _____

19. $5 + 5 =$ _____

20. $3 + 6 =$ _____

21. $4 + 2 =$ _____

22. $7 + 3 =$ _____

23. $2 + 3 =$ _____

24. $3 + 3 =$ _____

25. $4 + 5 =$ _____

26. $10 + 0 =$ _____

27. $2 + 1 =$ _____

28. $8 + 2 =$ _____

29. $2 + 7 =$ _____

30. $8 + 1 =$ _____

31. $3 + 4 =$ _____

32. $3 + 7 =$ _____

33. $4 + 3 =$ _____

34. $6 + 4 =$ _____

35. $7 + 0 =$ _____

36. $4 + 6 =$ _____

37. $5 + 1 =$ _____

38. $6 + 1 =$ _____

39. $5 + 2 =$ _____

40. $0 + 10 =$ _____

41. 7 minus 4 = _____

42. 6 minus 4 = _____

43. 9 minus 4 = _____

44. 7 minus 3 = _____

45. 10 minus 4 = _____

46. 4 minus 4 = _____

47. 8 minus 4 = _____

48. 6 minus 3 = _____

49. 10 minus 3 = _____

50. 5 minus 4 = _____

Here are the Chinese numerals from one to ten. Practice writing them on the lines. The Chinese do not have a symbol for "0."

1 = 一 _____

2 = 二 _____

3 = 三 _____

4 = 四 _____

5 = 五 _____

6 = 六 _____

7 = 七 _____

8 = 八 _____

9 = 九 _____

10 = 十 _____

My score: _____ My time: _____ min _____ s

The main thing I didn't understand was _____.

I now know that _____

_____.

I'm happy   I'm not happy   OOPS!   I didn't understand

Find the sum of...

1. 3 and 6 = _____

2. 9 and 1 = _____

3. 1 and 8 = _____

4. 3 and 5 = _____

5. 6 and 4 = _____

6. 1 and 7 = _____

7. 6 and 3 = _____

8. 0 and 10 = _____

9. 8 and 1 = _____

10. 5 and 5 = _____

11. 5 and 3 = _____

12. 7 and 1 = _____

13. 3 and 7 = _____

14. 2 and 7 = _____

15. 10 and 0 = _____

16. 4 and 4 = _____

17. 7 and 3 = _____

18. 6 and 2 = _____

19. 0 and 9 = _____

20. 8 and 2 = _____

21. 3 and 4 = _____

22. 4 and 6 = _____

23. 2 and 8 = _____

24. 7 and 2 = _____

25. 5 and 4 = _____

26. 1 and 9 = _____

27. 2 and 6 = _____

28. 4 and 5 = _____

29. 3 and 2 = _____

30. 4 and 6 = _____

31. $10 - 2 =$ _____

32. $10 - 1 =$ _____

33. $10 - 5 =$ _____

34. $10 - 8 =$ _____

35. $10 - 6 =$ _____

36. $10 - 10 =$ _____

37. $10 - 9 =$ _____

38. $10 - 7 =$ _____

39. $10 - 4 =$ _____

40. $10 - 3 =$ _____

41. $9 - 6 =$ _____

42. $8 - 7 =$ _____

43. $10 - 7 =$ _____

44. $8 - 5 =$ _____

45. $6 - 4 =$ _____

46. $4 - 3 =$ _____

47. $9 - 7 =$ _____

48. $7 - 5 =$ _____

49. $6 - 5 =$ _____

50. $8 - 6 =$ _____

Number or Numeral?

Bruce is from Australia, Jim is from outer space, Omar is from China and Claudius is from ancient Rome. When the teacher asked them to think of three birds, each closed his eyes and pictured this...

They wrote how many birds they saw in their books. Bruce wrote 3, Jim wrote L, Omar wrote ☰ and Claudius wrote III.

Each had written different numerals that stood for the same number.

The number is the idea, the numeral is the way we write it down.

My score: _____ My time: _____ min _____ s

The main thing I didn't understand was _____.

I now know that _____

_____.

1. 5 + 5 = _____

2. 2 + 8 = _____

3. 6 + 3 = _____

4. 6 + 4 = _____

5. 3 + 4 = _____

6. 3 + 5 = _____

7. 8 + 2 = _____

8. 3 + 2 = _____

9. 4 + 4 = _____

10. 7 + 2 = _____

11. 1 + 3 = _____

12. 2 + 6 = _____

13. 4 + 3 = _____

14. 1 + 9 = _____

15. 4 + 5 = _____

16. 2 + 5 = _____

17. 6 + 2 = _____

18. 3 + 7 = _____

19. 3 + 6 = _____

20. 9 + 1 = _____

21. 5 + 2 = _____

22. 7 + 3 = _____

23. 6 + 1 = _____

24. 3 + 7 = _____

25. 5 + 4 = _____

26. 4 + 6 = _____

27. 1 + 6 = _____

28. 2 + 7 = _____

29. 1 + 8 = _____

30. 5 + 3 = _____

31. 10 – 8 = _____

32. 8 – 6 = _____

33. 10 – 3 = _____

34. 9 – 8 = _____

35. 3 – 3 = _____

36. 9 – 7 = _____

37. 8 – 7 = _____

38. 10 – 9 = _____

39. 2 – 1 = _____

40. 10 – 7 = _____

41. 20 + 3 = _____

42. 20 + 6 = _____

43. 20 + 4 = _____

44. 20 + 7 = _____

45. 20 + 9 = _____

46. 30 + 4 = _____

47. 30 + 8 = _____

48. 30 + 5 = _____

49. 30 + 1 = _____

50. 30 + 0 = _____

What is the missing number?

(It is the same in all cases.)

_____ Dwarfs   _____ Seas

_____ Wonders of the World

Practice writing the Chinese

numeral for one on the lines.

_____

_____

My score: _____   My time: _____ min _____ s

The main thing I didn't understand was _____.

I now know that _____

_____.

1. 1 + 8 =	26. 3 + 6 =	51. 3 + 4 =	76. 2 + 5 =
2. 4 + 1 =	27. 4 + 3 =	52. 2 + 7 =	77. 5 + 2 =
3. 2 + 0 =	28. 5 + 0 =	53. 5 + 3 =	78. 3 + 4 =
4. 1 + 7 =	29. 1 + 5 =	54. 3 + 5 =	79. 7 + 1 =
5. 8 + 1 =	30. 4 + 1 =	55. 4 + 2 =	80. 2 + 2 =
6. 6 + 1 =	31. 1 + 4 =	56. 5 + 1 =	81. 1 + 3 =
7. 2 + 1 =	32. 6 + 2 =	57. 3 + 5 =	82. 8 + 0 =
8. 5 + 1 =	33. 4 + 2 =	58. 1 + 6 =	83. 5 + 3 =
9. 7 + 1 =	34. 2 + 6 =	59. 7 + 2 =	84. 7 + 2 =
10. 1 + 6 =	35. 5 + 2 =	60. 0 + 6 =	85. 3 + 5 =
11. 2 + 2 =	36. 2 + 5 =	61. 2 + 4 =	86. 5 + 3 =
12. 2 + 6 =	37. 4 + 3 =	62. 3 + 6 =	87. 4 + 5 =
13. 1 + 0 =	38. 6 + 1 =	63. 8 + 1 =	88. 6 + 0 =
14. 0 + 3 =	39. 1 + 5 =	64. 2 + 1 =	89. 5 + 4 =
15. 3 + 2 =	40. 5 + 4 =	65. 6 + 2 =	90. 4 + 0 =
16. 2 + 3 =	41. 3 + 0 =	66. 6 + 3 =	91. 3 + 1 =
17. 2 + 7 =	42. 5 + 4 =	67. 3 + 2 =	92. 0 + 9 =
18. 7 + 2 =	43. 4 + 5 =	68. 2 + 3 =	93. 2 + 7 =
19. 0 + 4 =	44. 1 + 1 =	69. 1 + 4 =	94. 3 + 3 =
20. 1 + 2 =	45. 3 + 1 =	70. 0 + 7 =	95. 9 + 0 =
21. 2 + 1 =	46. 4 + 4 =	71. 0 + 8 =	96. 1 + 8 =
22. 3 + 4 =	47. 5 + 4 =	72. 4 + 3 =	97. 2 + 4 =
23. 5 + 3 =	48. 4 + 4 =	73. 7 + 0 =	98. 1 + 3 =
24. 0 + 5 =	49. 1 + 1 =	74. 0 + 1 =	99. 3 + 3 =
25. 6 + 3 =	50. 0 + 2 =	75. 1 + 7 =	100. 1 + 9 =

My score: _____ My time: _____ min _____ s

The main thing I didn't understand was _____.

I now know that _____

_____

1.　4 + 2 = _____
2.　2 + 4 = _____
3.　3 + 5 = _____
4.　8 + 1 = _____
5.　2 + 1 = _____
6.　0 + 10 = _____
7.　3 + 3 = _____
8.　1 + 5 = _____
9.　2 + 5 = _____
10.　0 + 6 = _____
11.　4 + 3 = _____
12.　2 + 8 = _____
13.　5 + 3 = _____
14.　2 + 2 = _____
15.　3 + 5 = _____
16.　7 + 1 = _____
17.　0 + 8 = _____
18.　4 + 1 = _____
19.　1 + 4 = _____
20.　5 + 3 = _____
21.　4 + 4 = _____
22.　0 + 5 = _____
23.　1 + 9 = _____
24.　5 + 0 = _____
25.　6 + 2 = _____

26.　2 + 3 = _____
27.　3 + 2 = _____
28.　6 + 2 = _____
29.　6 + 4 = _____
30.　3 + 7 = _____
31.　2 + 6 = _____
32.　7 + 3 = _____
33.　5 + 5 = _____
34.　4 + 5 = _____
35.　7 + 3 = _____
36.　3 + 7 = _____
37.　4 + 4 = _____
38.　2 + 7 = _____
39.　8 + 2 = _____
40.　7 + 2 = _____
41.　10 + 0 = _____
42.　1 + 2 = _____
43.　1 + 8 = _____
44.　5 + 1 = _____
45.　0 + 9 = _____
46.　6 + 0 = _____
47.　4 + 6 = _____
48.　5 + 2 = _____
49.　4 + 5 = _____
50.　3 + 4 = _____

51.　4 + 6 = _____
52.　8 + 2 = _____
53.　1 + 7 = _____
54.　3 + 5 = _____
55.　8 + 0 = _____
56.　2 + 6 = _____
57.　3 + 4 = _____
58.　9 + 1 = _____
59.　4 + 6 = _____
60.　9 + 0 = _____
61.　10 − 2 = _____
62.　9 − 3 = _____
63.　10 − 8 = _____
64.　9 − 4 = _____
65.　10 − 3 = _____
66.　7 − 4 = _____
67.　8 − 3 = _____
68.　8 − 5 = _____
69.　10 − 5 = _____
70.　7 − 5 = _____
71.　6 − 3 = _____
72.　8 − 4 = _____
73.　7 − 1 = _____
74.　10 − 7 = _____
75.　6 − 4 = _____

76.　7 − 6 = _____
77.　10 − 6 = _____
78.　5 − 3 = _____
79.　9 − 9 = _____
80.　8 − 1 = _____
81.　9 − 0 = _____
82.　7 − 3 = _____
83.　10 − 1 = _____
84.　8 − 0 = _____
85.　9 − 1 = _____
86.　7 − 7 = _____
87.　9 − 8 = _____
88.　9 − 2 = _____
89.　10 − 0 = _____
90.　9 − 7 = _____
91.　10 − 9 = _____
92.　8 − 8 = _____
93.　9 − 6 = _____
94.　10 − 10 = _____
95.　7 − 2 = _____
96.　8 − 7 = _____
97.　8 − 2 = _____
98.　9 − 5 = _____
99.　10 − 4 = _____
100.　8 − 6 = _____

My score: _____　　My time: _____ min _____ s

The main thing I didn't understand was _____.

I now know that _____

_____.

11 + 0 = 11

10 + 1 = 11

9 + 2 = 11

8 + 3 = 11

7 + 4 = 11

6 + 5 = 11

5 + 6 = 11

4 + 7 = 11

3 + 8 = 11

2 + 9 = 11

1 + 10 = 11

0 + 11 = 11

11 – 0 = 11

11 – 1 = 10

11 – 2 = 9

11 – 3 = 8

11 – 4 = 7

11 – 5 = 6

11 – 6 = 5

11 – 7 = 4

11 – 8 = 3

11 – 9 = 2

11 – 10 = 1

11 – 11 = 0

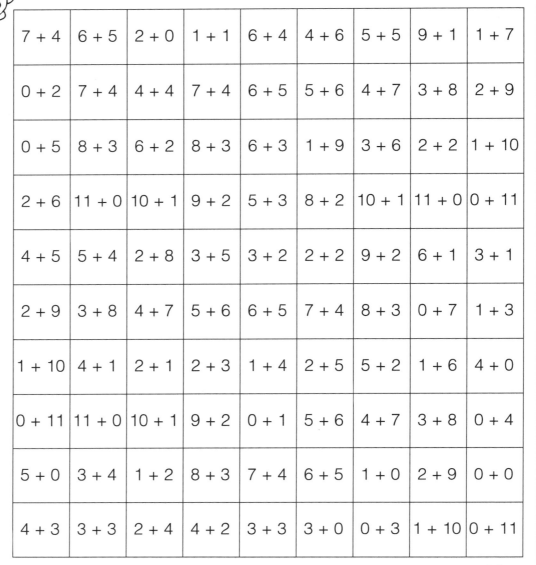

7 + 4	6 + 5	2 + 0	1 + 1	6 + 4	4 + 6	5 + 5	9 + 1	1 + 7
0 + 2	7 + 4	4 + 4	7 + 4	6 + 5	5 + 6	4 + 7	3 + 8	2 + 9
0 + 5	8 + 3	6 + 2	8 + 3	6 + 3	1 + 9	3 + 6	2 + 2	1 + 10
2 + 6	11 + 0	10 + 1	9 + 2	5 + 3	8 + 2	10 + 1	11 + 0	0 + 11
4 + 5	5 + 4	2 + 8	3 + 5	3 + 2	2 + 2	9 + 2	6 + 1	3 + 1
2 + 9	3 + 8	4 + 7	5 + 6	6 + 5	7 + 4	8 + 3	0 + 7	1 + 3
1 + 10	4 + 1	2 + 1	2 + 3	1 + 4	2 + 5	5 + 2	1 + 6	4 + 0
0 + 11	11 + 0	10 + 1	9 + 2	0 + 1	5 + 6	4 + 7	3 + 8	0 + 4
5 + 0	3 + 4	1 + 2	8 + 3	7 + 4	6 + 5	1 + 0	2 + 9	0 + 0
4 + 3	3 + 3	2 + 4	4 + 2	3 + 3	3 + 0	0 + 3	1 + 10	0 + 11

Bruce is going over to Alison's house to talk about the weather and his string collection.

He is going to follow the path made by all the squares that add up to eleven. Color this path and show the way he goes. You can only travel up, down and across, not diagonally.

Did you know the sun rises in the east and sets in the west?

My score: _____ My time: _____ min _____ s

The main thing I didn't understand was _____.

I now know that _____
_____.

1. 6 + 4 = _____
2. 3 + 6 = _____
3. 4 + 7 = _____
4. 5 + 5 = _____
5. 2 + 6 = _____
6. 11 + 0 = _____
7. 2 + 4 = _____
8. 2 + 3 = _____
9. 4 + 7 = _____
10. 5 + 2 = _____
11. 2 + 8 = _____
12. 3 + 8 = _____
13. 5 + 3 = _____
14. 7 + 4 = _____
15. 8 + 3 = _____
16. 10 + 1 = _____
17. 4 + 6 = _____

18. 4 + 3 = _____
19. 5 + 6 = _____
20. 3 + 7 = _____
21. 3 + 5 = _____
22. 0 + 11 = _____
23. 4 + 5 = _____
24. 2 + 7 = _____
25. 1 + 10 = _____
26. 7 + 3 = _____
27. 3 + 2 = _____
28. 2 + 9 = _____
29. 4 + 7 = _____
30. 5 + 6 = _____
31. 6 + 3 = _____
32. 9 + 2 = _____
33. 3 + 4 = _____
34. 8 + 2 = _____

35. 5 + 4 = _____
36. 6 + 5 = _____
37. 4 + 4 = _____
38. 7 + 4 = _____
39. 2 + 5 = _____
40. 4 + 2 = _____
41. 10 + 10 = _____
42. 20 + 10 = _____
43. 30 + 20 = _____
44. 20 + 20 = _____
45. 40 + 20 = _____
46. 30 + 40 = _____
47. 40 + 40 = _____
48. 30 + 40 = _____
49. 60 + 20 = _____
50. 20 + 40 = _____

What is the missing number?
(It is the same in both cases.)

_____ players on a softball team

someone all dressed to the _____s

Practice writing the Chinese
numeral for two on the lines.

_____

_____

My score: _____ My time: _____ min _____ s

The main thing I didn't understand was _____.

I now know that _____

_____.

1.　4 + 3 = _____

2.　8 + 2 = _____

3.　1 + 10 = _____

4.　4 + 4 = _____

5.　4 + 6 = _____

6.　2 + 9 = _____

7.　2 + 8 = _____

8.　6 + 3 = _____

9.　10 + 0 = _____

10.　5 + 6 = _____

11.　8 + 3 = _____

12.　9 + 1 = _____

13.　6 + 5 = _____

14.　0 + 10 = _____

15.　6 + 5 = _____

16.　3 + 4 = _____

17.　5 + 6 = _____

18.　3 + 6 = _____

19.　3 + 8 = _____

20.　5 + 3 = _____

21.　7 + 3 = _____

22.　4 + 7 = _____

23.　1 + 9 = _____

24.　9 + 2 = _____

25.　4 + 3 = _____

26.　3 + 8 = _____

27.　4 + 7 = _____

28.　4 + 5 = _____

29.　0 + 11 = _____

30.　5 + 4 = _____

31.　7 + 4 = _____

32.　3 + 7 = _____

33.　3 + 5 = _____

34.　8 + 3 = _____

35.　5 + 5 = _____

36.　10 + 1 = _____

37.　4 + 6 = _____

38.　7 + 4 = _____

39.　11 + 0 = _____

40.　6 + 4 = _____

41.　11 less 4 = _____

42.　11 less 8 = _____

43.　11 less 5 = _____

44.　11 less 1 = _____

45.　11 less 7 = _____

46.　11 less 2 = _____

47.　11 less 9 = _____

48.　11 less 6 = _____

49.　11 less 10 = _____

50.　11 less 3 = _____

Farmer Blue said, "I had two ducks in front of a duck and two ducks behind a duck and one duck in the middle."

"I had the smallest number of ducks I could have for this to be true."

What is the smallest number of ducks? Circle the right row of ducks.

My score: _____ My time: _____ min _____ s

The main thing I didn't understand was _____.

I now know that _____
_____

Subtract...

1. 3 from 11 = _____

2. 6 from 11 = _____

3. 10 from 11 = _____

4. 4 from 11 = _____

5. 7 from 11 = _____

6. 11 from 11 = _____

7. 5 from 11 = _____

8. 8 from 11 = _____

9. 9 from 11 = _____

10. 2 from 11 = _____

11. 2 + 9 = _____

12. 3 + 7 = _____

13. 1 + 10 = _____

14. 4 + 5 = _____

15. 6 + 5 = _____

16. 4 + 3 = _____

17. 4 + 6 = _____

18. 4 + 7 = _____

19. 3 + 6 = _____

20. 2 + 3 = _____

21. 7 + 3 = _____

22. 5 + 6 = _____

23. 7 + 4 = _____

24. 3 + 2 = _____

25. 9 + 2 = _____

26. 6 + 4 = _____

27. 5 + 3 = _____

28. 8 + 3 = _____

29. 0 + 11 = _____

30. 9 + 1 = _____

31. 2 + 8 = _____

32. 3 + 8 = _____

33. 6 + 3 = _____

34. 3 + 4 = _____

35. 10 + 1 = _____

36. 5 + 4 = _____

37. 2 + 7 = _____

38. 8 + 2 = _____

39. 5 + 6 = _____

40. 8 + 3 = _____

41. 18 + 3 = _____

42. 28 + 3 = _____

43. 38 + 3 = _____

44. 48 + 3 = _____

45. 58 + 3 = _____

46. 68 + 3 = _____

47. 78 + 3 = _____

48. 88 + 3 = _____

49. 98 + 3 = _____

50. Days in a week = ____

"Tri" in front of a word often stands for three.

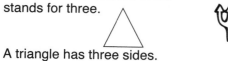

A triangle has three sides.

A tricycle has three wheels.

A trident has three prongs.

A tripod has three legs.

You might even be a triplet like these babies.

My score: _____ My time: _____ min _____ s

The main thing I didn't understand was _____.

I now know that _____

_____

Math Speed Tests – Book 1

1. 2 plus 8 = _____

2. 8 plus 3 = _____

3. 4 plus 6 = _____

4. 5 plus 4 = _____

5. 10 plus 1 = _____

6. 3 plus 5 = _____

7. 4 plus 7 = _____

8. 6 plus 4 = _____

9. 4 plus 4 = _____

10. 5 plus 6 = _____

11. 4 plus 5 = _____

12. 5 plus 3 = _____

13. 6 plus 5 = _____

14. 4 plus 3 = _____

15. 5 plus 5 = _____

16. 2 plus 4 = _____

17. 7 plus 4 = _____

18. 2 plus 7 = _____

19. 3 plus 7 = _____

20. 4 plus 7 = _____

21. 2 plus 6 = _____

22. 3 plus 4 = _____

23. 3 plus 8 = _____

24. 6 plus 3 = _____

25. 2 plus 9 = _____

26. 7 plus 3 = _____

27. 9 plus 2 = _____

28. 2 plus 3 = _____

29. 3 plus 6 = _____

30. 7 plus 2 = _____

31. $10 - 3 =$ _____

32. $11 - 3 =$ _____

33. $9 - 3 =$ _____

34. $7 - 3 =$ _____

35. $8 - 3 =$ _____

36. $4 - 3 =$ _____

37. $6 - 3 =$ _____

38. $5 - 3 =$ _____

39. $11 - 8 =$ _____

40. $11 - 2 =$ _____

41. $30 + 2 =$ _____

42. $70 + 1 =$ _____

43. $10 + 5 =$ _____

44. $40 + 7 =$ _____

45. $80 + 3 =$ _____

46. $60 + 5 =$ _____

47. $50 + 8 =$ _____

48. $40 + 2 =$ _____

49. $20 + 4 =$ _____

50. $60 + 9 =$ _____

Practice writing the Chinese numeral for three on the lines.

三

_____

_____

Tip The order that you add numbers makes no difference to your answer.

For example, 7 + 2 = 9 and 2 + 7 = 9

You will find it faster to add the smaller number to the bigger number in your mind.

My score: _____ My time: _____ min _____ s

The main thing I didn't understand was _____.

I now know that _____

_____.

1. 5 + 5 = _____
2. 4 + 7 = _____
3. 6 + 4 = _____
4. 5 + 6 = _____
5. 7 + 3 = _____
6. 10 + 1 = _____
7. 0 + 10 = _____
8. 11 + 0 = _____
9. 8 + 2 = _____
10. 6 + 5 = _____
11. 1 + 9 = _____
12. 7 + 4 = _____
13. 6 + 3 = _____
14. 2 + 8 = _____
15. 9 + 1 = _____
16. 8 + 3 = _____
17. 3 + 7 = _____
18. 5 + 4 = _____
19. 10 + 0 = _____
20. 4 + 6 = _____
21. 9 + 2 = _____
22. 4 + 5 = _____
23. 0 + 11 = _____
24. 1 + 8 = _____
25. 1 + 10 = _____

26. 3 + 6 = _____
27. 2 + 9 = _____
28. 2 + 7 = _____
29. 3 + 8 = _____
30. 0 + 9 = _____
31. 1 + 10 = _____
32. 6 + 4 = _____
33. 2 + 8 = _____
34. 5 + 6 = _____
35. 4 + 6 = _____
36. 6 + 5 = _____
37. 2 + 9 = _____
38. 7 + 4 = _____
39. 8 + 3 = _____
40. 7 + 3 = _____
41. 0 + 10 = _____
42. 3 + 7 = _____
43. 3 + 8 = _____
44. 4 + 7 = _____
45. 0 + 11 = _____
46. 8 + 2 = _____
47. 5 + 6 = _____
48. 1 + 9 = _____
49. 5 + 5 = _____
50. 9 + 2 = _____

51. 2 + 5 = _____
52. 4 + 5 = _____
53. 6 + 5 = _____
54. 5 + 6 = _____
55. 3 + 4 = _____
56. 4 + 3 = _____
57. 4 + 6 = _____
58. 6 + 4 = _____
59. 5 + 4 = _____
60. 5 + 3 = _____
61. 3 + 7 = _____
62. 0 + 11 = _____
63. 2 + 2 = _____
64. 3 + 2 = _____
65. 11 + 0 = _____
66. 5 + 6 = _____
67. 6 + 5 = _____
68. 3 + 3 = _____
69. 4 + 2 = _____
70. 4 + 7 = _____
71. 5 + 2 = _____
72. 7 + 4 = _____
73. 3 + 6 = _____
74. 6 + 2 = _____
75. 8 + 3 = _____

76. 3 + 8 = _____
77. 3 + 4 = _____
78. 3 + 5 = _____
79. 2 + 9 = _____
80. 9 + 2 = _____
81. 4 + 6 = _____
82. 4 + 2 = _____
83. 8 + 3 = _____
84. 4 + 5 = _____
85. 4 + 1 = _____
86. 7 + 4 = _____
87. 4 + 4 = _____
88. 4 + 7 = _____
89. 4 + 3 = _____
90. 3 + 7 = _____
91. 20 + 4 = _____
92. 30 + 5 = _____
93. 40 + 7 = _____
94. 20 + 8 = _____
95. 30 + 8 = _____
96. 20 + 6 = _____
97. 40 + 1 = _____
98. 30 + 9 = _____
99. 20 + 7 = _____
100. 30 + 2 = _____

My score: _____ My time: _____ min _____ s

The main thing I didn't understand was _____.

I now know that _____

_____

12 + 0 = 12
11 + 1 = 12
10 + 2 = 12
9 + 3 = 12
8 + 4 = 12
7 + 5 = 12
6 + 6 = 12
5 + 7 = 12
4 + 8 = 12
3 + 9 = 12
2 + 10 = 12
1 + 11 = 12
0 + 12 = 12

12 − 0 = 12
12 − 1 = 11
12 − 2 = 10
12 − 3 = 9
12 − 4 = 8
12 − 5 = 7
12 − 6 = 6
12 − 7 = 5
12 − 8 = 4
12 − 9 = 3
12 − 10 = 2
12 − 11 = 1
12 − 12 = 0

7 + 5	7 + 2	6 + 5	4 + 4	5 + 2	2 + 5	2 + 5	3 + 2	5 + 6
5 + 7	4 + 0	5 + 3	3 + 7	4 + 6	8 + 3	3 + 8	6 + 5	3 + 4
6 + 6	1 + 6	6 + 6	10 + 2	2 + 10	4 + 7	7 + 4	4 + 5	1 + 3
9 + 3	8 + 4	7 + 5	2 + 6	11 + 1	1 + 11	10 + 2	2 + 10	2 + 4
1 + 8	4 + 4	5 + 3	3 + 5	6 + 2	2 + 6	4 + 7	3 + 9	5 + 2
8 + 1	12 + 0	6 + 6	5 + 7	7 + 5	8 + 4	4 + 8	9 + 3	4 + 2
9 + 1	0 + 12	1 + 9	0 + 10	10 + 0	3 + 6	6 + 3	7 + 2	3 + 3
7 + 3	11 + 1	8 + 2	9 + 3	3 + 9	4 + 8	6 + 6	2 + 7	4 + 3
3 + 7	1 + 11	2 + 10	10 + 2	2 + 9	8 + 3	5 + 7	9 + 2	5 + 4
5 + 5	6 + 4	4 + 6	1 + 10	10 + 1	3 + 8	7 + 5	6 + 6	8 + 4

Bruce and his friends won a trip to Twelveland. Here they are at Twelveland's large airport. It is a big place and they would be happy if you could help.

The quickest way out is by following the squares that add up to twelve.

Color them to find their way. You can only travel up, down and across, not diagonally.

My score: _____ My time: _____ min _____ s

The main thing I didn't understand was _____.

I now know that _____
_____.

1. 4 + 5 = _____

2. 10 + 2 = _____

3. 5 + 6 = _____

4. 3 + 7 = _____

5. 11 + 1 = _____

6. 3 + 5 = _____

7. 7 + 4 = _____

8. 4 + 7 = _____

9. 0 + 12 = _____

10. 5 + 3 = _____

11. 5 + 7 = _____

12. 7 + 3 = _____

13. 6 + 3 = _____

14. 3 + 4 = _____

15. 4 + 8 = _____

16. 3 + 9 = _____

17. 6 + 5 = _____

18. 12 + 0 = _____

19. 6 + 4 = _____

20. 4 + 8 = _____

21. 2 + 4 = _____

22. 5 + 7 = _____

23. 3 + 8 = _____

24. 3 + 6 = _____

25. 6 + 6 = _____

26. 5 + 6 = _____

27. 7 + 5 = _____

28. 5 + 4 = _____

29. 4 + 3 = _____

30. 8 + 4 = _____

31. 9 + 3 = _____

32. 6 + 5 = _____

33. 5 + 7 = _____

34. 7 + 5 = _____

35. 4 + 6 = _____

36. 2 + 10 = _____

37. 2 + 5 = _____

38. 8 + 4 = _____

39. 8 + 3 = _____

40. 1 + 11 = _____

Difference between...

41. 12 and 1 = _____

42. 3 and 6 = _____

43. 2 and 12 = _____

44. 12 and 7 = _____

45. 12 and 6 = _____

46. 4 and 12 = _____

47. 12 and 9 = _____

48. 5 and 12 = _____

49. 8 and 12 = _____

50. 12 and 3 = _____

Difference

Farmer Bloggs has two fields with sheep in them.

In the first field there are two sheep and in the second field there are five sheep.

Each field has a first sheep (1) and a second sheep (2) but only the second field has a third, fourth and fifth sheep.

The three extra sheep are the difference.
The difference between 5 and 2 is 3.

In mathematics we find the difference by subtracting.

My score: _____ My time: _____ min _____ s

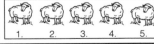

The main thing I didn't understand was _____.

I now know that _____

_____.

1.　2 + 9 = _____

2.　8 + 4 = _____

3.　6 + 4 = _____

4.　11 + 1 = _____

5.　4 + 6 = _____

6.　2 + 9 = _____

7.　3 + 7 = _____

8.　6 + 3 = _____

9.　4 + 7 = _____

10.　4 + 2 = _____

11.　4 + 8 = _____

12.　1 + 3 = _____

13.　8 + 4 = _____

14.　7 + 4 = _____

15.　3 + 9 = _____

16.　7 + 3 = _____

17.　9 + 3 = _____

18.　4 + 4 = _____

19.　0 + 12 = _____

20.　5 + 4 = _____

21.　2 + 4 = _____

22.　3 + 8 = _____

23.　5 + 7 = _____

24.　5 + 3 = _____

25.　2 + 5 = _____

26.　12 + 0 = _____

27.　7 + 5 = _____

28.　4 + 5 = _____

29.　10 + 2 = _____

30.　3 + 5 = _____

31.　2 + 6 = _____

32.　1 + 11 = _____

33.　5 + 7 = _____

34.　3 + 6 = _____

35.　6 + 6 = _____

36.　3 + 4 = _____

37.　2 + 8 = _____

38.　7 + 5 = _____

39.　6 + 6 = _____

40.　4 + 3 = _____

41.　20 + 7 = _____

42.　50 + 7 = _____

43.　10 + 7 = _____

44.　40 + 7 = _____

45.　30 + 7 = _____

46.　70 + 7 = _____

47.　80 + 7 = _____

48.　100 + 7 = _____

49.　90 + 7 = _____

50.　60 + 7 = _____

What is the missing number? (It is the same in all cases.)

_____ eggs come in a regular carton. _____ is a dozen.

_____ lots of a dozen is called a gross (144).

Practice writing the Chinese numeral for four on the lines. 四

_____

_____

My score: _____　My time: _____ min _____ s

The main thing I didn't understand was _____ .

I now know that _____
_____ .

1. 6 + 5 = _____

2. 9 + 3 = _____

3. 3 + 7 = _____

4. 0 + 12 = _____

5. 4 + 7 = _____

6. 8 + 4 = _____

7. 7 + 3 = _____

8. 12 + 0 = _____

9. 4 + 6 = _____

10. 7 + 5 = _____

11. 2 + 5 = _____

12. 7 + 4 = _____

13. 11 + 1 = _____

14. 5 + 7 = _____

15. 3 + 8 = _____

16. 6 + 4 = _____

17. 1 + 11 = _____

18. 8 + 3 = _____

19. 3 + 5 = _____

20. 2 + 10 = _____

21. 4 + 3 = _____

22. 6 + 6 = _____

23. 5 + 4 = _____

24. 10 + 2 = _____

25. 3 + 6 = _____

26. 3 + 9 = _____

27. 5 + 6 = _____

28. 4 + 8 = _____

29. 4 + 5 = _____

30. 9 + 2 = _____

31. 12 – 0 = _____

32. 12 – 4 = _____

33. 12 – 8 = _____

34. 12 – 9 = _____

35. 12 – 2 = _____

36. 12 – 5 = _____

37. 12 – 3 = _____

38. 12 – 7 = _____

39. 12 – 6 = _____

40. 12 – 1 = _____

41. 7 + 5 = _____

42. 17 + 5 = _____

43. 27 + 5 = _____

44. 37 + 5 = _____

45. 47 + 5 = _____

46. 57 + 5 = _____

47. 67 + 5 = _____

48. 77 + 5 = _____

49. 87 + 5 = _____

50. 97 + 5 = _____

Practice writing the Chinese numeral for five on the lines. 五

_____

_____

There is an old saying that "four noses are better than three," but nobody has ever proved it.

My score: _____ My time: _____ min _____ s

The main thing I didn't understand was _____.

I now know that _____

_____.

Write the sum of...

1. 2 and 10 = _____

2. 5 and 5 = _____

3. 6 and 5 = _____

4. 1 and 11 = _____

5. 5 and 4 = _____

6. 4 and 3 = _____

7. 4 and 8 = _____

8. 8 and 4 = _____

9. 4 and 6 = _____

10. 4 and 7 = _____

11. 9 and 3 = _____

12. 6 and 4 = _____

13. 5 and 7 = _____

14. 7 and 4 = _____

15. 6 and 6 = _____

16. 3 and 7 = _____

17. 3 and 9 = _____

18. 3 and 8 = _____

19. 7 and 5 = _____

20. 5 and 3 = _____

21. 10 and 2 = _____

22. 2 and 3 = _____

23. 3 and 6 = _____

24. 4 and 5 = _____

25. 3 and 4 = _____

26. 5 and 6 = _____

27. 11 and 1 = _____

28. 7 and 3 = _____

29. 8 and 3 = _____

30. 3 and 2 = _____

31. 2 + 3 + 4 = _____

32. 3 + 2 + 3 = _____

33. 3 + 4 + 5 = _____

34. 5 + 2 + 3 = _____

35. 4 + 3 + 3 = _____

36. 4 + 1 + 3 = _____

37. 5 + 1 + 6 = _____

38. 2 + 4 + 3 = _____

39. 3 + 8 + 0 = _____

40. 2 + 3 + 1 = _____

41. 12 − 9 = _____

42. 11 − 8 = _____

43. 12 − 4 = _____

44. 12 − 8 = _____

45. 10 − 6 = _____

46. 12 − 10 = _____

47. 11 − 6 = _____

48. 12 − 7 = _____

49. 12 − 5 = _____

50. 12 − 6 = _____

"Cent" as part of a word often has something to do with one hundred.

100 cents = $1.00, 100 years = a century

100 centimeters = 1 meter. A centurion was a soldier in Rome in charge of 100 men.

Practice writing the Chinese numeral for six on the lines.

六 _____

_____

My score: _____ My time: _____ min _____ s

The main thing I didn't understand was _____.

I now know that _____

_____

1. 0 + 9 = _____	26. 2 + 10 = _____	51. 0 + 12 = _____	76. 8 + 3 = _____
2. 3 + 6 = _____	27. 9 + 0 = _____	52. 0 + 9 = _____	77. 7 + 4 = _____
3. 0 + 12 = _____	28. 10 + 0 = _____	53. 3 + 8 = _____	78. 9 + 2 = _____
4. 12 + 0 = _____	29. 8 + 2 = _____	54. 9 + 1 = _____	79. 11 + 0 = _____
5. 2 + 7 = _____	30. 6 + 4 = _____	55. 1 + 9 = _____	80. 8 + 4 = _____
6. 6 + 6 = _____	31. 4 + 6 = _____	56. 2 + 8 = _____	81. 0 + 11 = _____
7. 9 + 0 = _____	32. 7 + 3 = _____	57. 10 + 2 = _____	82. 4 + 8 = _____
8. 7 + 2 = _____	33. 1 + 11 = _____	58. 2 + 10 = _____	83. 5 + 7 = _____
9. 6 + 3 = _____	34. 11 + 1 = _____	59. 5 + 5 = _____	84. 10 + 1 = _____
10. 6 + 6 = _____	35. 8 + 1 = _____	60. 8 + 2 = _____	85. 7 + 5 = _____
11. 8 + 1 = _____	36. 1 + 8 = _____	61. 10 + 0 = _____	86. 4 + 7 = _____
12. 5 + 7 = _____	37. 2 + 8 = _____	62. 8 + 3 = _____	87. 0 + 11 = _____
13. 7 + 5 = _____	38. 0 + 10 = _____	63. 9 + 3 = _____	88. 9 + 2 = _____
14. 1 + 8 = _____	39. 8 + 4 = _____	64. 3 + 9 = _____	89. 2 + 9 = _____
15. 4 + 5 = _____	40. 4 + 8 = _____	65. 0 + 10 = _____	90. 5 + 7 = _____
16. 5 + 4 = _____	41. 3 + 7 = _____	66. 5 + 5 = _____	91. 9 + 3 = _____
17. 4 + 8 = _____	42. 7 + 2 = _____	67. 5 + 6 = _____	92. 10 + 1 = _____
18. 8 + 4 = _____	43. 9 + 1 = _____	68. 6 + 4 = _____	93. 4 + 3 = _____
19. 6 + 3 = _____	44. 5 + 7 = _____	69. 2 + 9 = _____	94. 6 + 5 = _____
20. 5 + 4 = _____	45. 7 + 5 = _____	70. 6 + 5 = _____	95. 5 + 6 = _____
21. 3 + 6 = _____	46. 2 + 7 = _____	71. 4 + 6 = _____	96. 1 + 10 = _____
22. 9 + 3 = _____	47. 11 + 1 = _____	72. 1 + 10 = _____	97. 3 + 4 = _____
23. 3 + 9 = _____	48. 1 + 11 = _____	73. 3 + 8 = _____	98. 11 + 0 = _____
24. 4 + 5 = _____	49. 1 + 9 = _____	74. 7 + 3 = _____	99. 7 + 4 = _____
25. 10 + 2 = _____	50. 12 + 0 = _____	75. 3 + 7 = _____	100. 4 + 7 = _____

My score: _____ My time: _____ min _____ s

The main thing I didn't understand was _____.

I now know that _____

_____.

I'm happy

I'm not happy

OOPS!

I didn't understand

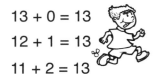

13 + 0 = 13
12 + 1 = 13
11 + 2 = 13
10 + 3 = 13
9 + 4 = 13
8 + 5 = 13
7 + 6 = 13
6 + 7 = 13
5 + 8 = 13
4 + 9 = 13
3 + 10 = 13
2 + 11 = 13
1 + 12 = 13
0 + 13 = 13

13 − 0 = 13
13 − 1 = 12
13 − 2 = 11
13 − 3 = 10
13 − 4 = 9
13 − 5 = 8
13 − 6 = 7
13 − 7 = 6
13 − 8 = 5
13 − 9 = 4
13 − 10 = 3
13 − 11 = 2
13 − 12 = 1
13 − 13 = 0

7 + 6	4 + 7	3 + 8	6 + 5	0 + 11	5 + 5	6 + 3	9 + 1	4 + 5
6 + 7	8 + 5	9 + 4	2 + 11	11 + 2	10 + 3	3 + 10	9 + 4	5 + 4
7 + 4	8 + 3	5 + 6	4 + 6	3 + 7	2 + 2	3 + 6	4 + 9	1 + 9
4 + 9	9 + 4	8 + 5	5 + 8	6 + 7	7 + 6	8 + 5	5 + 8	2 + 8
3 + 10	6 + 5	3 + 7	4 + 2	5 + 6	8 + 1	1 + 8	2 + 7	7 + 2
10 + 3	8 + 4	4 + 7	4 + 6	6 + 6	3 + 10	10 + 3	9 + 4	4 + 9
11 + 2	2 + 11	1 + 12	12 + 1	6 + 4	11 + 2	9 + 0	0 + 9	5 + 8
5 + 6	4 + 8	2 + 1	13 + 0	3 + 7	2 + 11	5 + 5	4 + 6	8 + 5
11 + 0	6 + 6	8 + 4	0 + 13	12 + 1	1 + 12	7 + 3	8 + 2	7 + 6
1 + 10	0 + 0	1 + 2	3 + 3	4 + 4	5 + 7	5 + 5	7 + 5	6 + 7

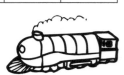

Jim is sprinting. He has to catch the thirteen minutes past one train (also called the 1:13).

Luckily there is a shortcut. By following the squares that add to thirteen he will be running downhill all the way.

Color them to show him the way. You can only travel up, down and across, not diagonally.

My score: _____ My time: _____ min _____ s

The main thing I didn't understand was _____.

I now know that _____

_____

1. $12 + 1 =$ _____
2. $3 + 8 =$ _____
3. $8 + 5 =$ _____
4. $4 + 8 =$ _____
5. $0 + 13 =$ _____
6. $9 + 2 =$ _____
7. $6 + 4 =$ _____
8. $9 + 3 =$ _____
9. $4 + 9 =$ _____
10. $7 + 5 =$ _____
11. $5 + 6 =$ _____
12. $4 + 6 =$ _____
13. $6 + 7 =$ _____
14. $7 + 6 =$ _____
15. $7 + 3 =$ _____
16. $10 + 3 =$ _____
17. $8 + 4 =$ _____

18. $1 + 12 =$ _____
19. $5 + 7 =$ _____
20. $8 + 3 =$ _____
21. $6 + 7 =$ _____
22. $7 + 6 =$ _____
23. $6 + 5 =$ _____
24. $4 + 5 =$ _____
25. $3 + 10 =$ _____
26. $3 + 7 =$ _____
27. $13 + 0 =$ _____
28. $6 + 6 =$ _____
29. $6 + 5 =$ _____
30. $4 + 5 =$ _____
31. $3 + 10 =$ _____
32. $5 + 8 =$ _____
33. $3 + 5 =$ _____
34. $5 + 7 =$ _____

35. $9 + 4 =$ _____
36. $7 + 5 =$ _____
37. $6 + 7 =$ _____
38. $2 + 9 =$ _____
39. $4 + 7 =$ _____
40. $2 + 11 =$ _____
41. $10 - 1 =$ _____
42. $60 - 1 =$ _____
43. $100 - 1 =$ _____
44. $90 - 1 =$ _____
45. $50 - 1 =$ _____
46. $30 - 1 =$ _____
47. $80 - 1 =$ _____
48. $40 - 1 =$ _____
49. $70 - 1 =$ _____
50. $20 - 1 =$ _____

Tallying is a way of writing an amount as you count it. Tallying is done in bundles of five. The first four are down strokes and the fifth is an across stroke.

Tally the number of children in your class.

‖‖‖	= 4
‖‖‖‖	= 5

Practice writing the Chinese numeral for seven on the lines.

 七 _____

_____

My score: _____   My time: _____ min _____ s

The main thing I didn't understand was _____.

I now know that _____

_____.

1. 6 + 6 = _____

2. 0 + 13 = _____

3. 6 + 5 = _____

4. 6 + 7 = _____

5. 5 + 5 = _____

6. 2 + 11 = _____

7. 7 + 6 = _____

8. 8 + 4 = _____

9. 4 + 6 = _____

10. 4 + 9 = _____

11. 4 + 7 = _____

12. 7 + 4 = _____

13. 4 + 8 = _____

14. 7 + 5 = _____

15. 6 + 7 = _____

16. 6 + 4 = _____

17. 7 + 4 = _____

18. 1 + 12 = _____

19. 5 + 6 = _____

20. 9 + 4 = _____

21. 3 + 7 = _____

22. 10 + 3 = _____

23. 6 + 7 = _____

24. 7 + 6 = _____

25. 7 + 3 = _____

26. 9 + 3 = _____

27. 5 + 8 = _____

28. 4 + 5 = _____

29. 11 + 2 = _____

30. 8 + 5 = _____

31. 5 + 7 = _____

32. 4 + 5 = _____

33. 12 + 1 = _____

34. 3 + 9 = _____

35. 8 + 5 = _____

36. 5 + 3 = _____

37. 3 + 10 = _____

38. 7 + 6 = _____

39. 3 + 5 = _____

40. 5 + 8 = _____

41. 13 – 1 = _____

42. 13 – 7 = _____

43. 13 – 4 = _____

44. 13 – 10 = _____

45. 13 – 5 = _____

46. 13 – 2 = _____

47. 13 – 8 = _____

48. 13 – 6 = _____

49. 13 – 9 = _____

50. 13 – 3 = _____

Make a tally of something.

Write the name of your tally.

A tally of _____.

Practice writing the Chinese numeral for eight on the lines.

_____

_____

My score: _____ My time: _____ min _____ s

The main thing I didn't understand was _____.

I now know that _____

_____

1. 6 + 7 = _____

2. 5 + 7 = _____

3. 13 + 0 = _____

4. 4 + 7 = _____

5. 1 + 12 = _____

6. 12 + 1 = _____

7. 4 + 6 = _____

8. 5 + 4 = _____

9. 11 + 2 = _____

10. 6 + 7 = _____

11. 4 + 5 = _____

12. 2 + 11 = _____

13. 6 + 6 = _____

14. 4 + 4 = _____

15. 5 + 5 = _____

16. 5 + 8 = _____

17. 8 + 5 = _____

18. 4 + 3 = _____

19. 5 + 2 = _____

20. 4 + 9 = _____

21. 6 + 5 = _____

22. 9 + 4 = _____

23. 6 + 4 = _____

24. 5 + 3 = _____

25. 10 + 3 = _____

26. 5 + 6 = _____

27. 4 + 8 = _____

28. 0 + 13 = _____

29. 7 + 6 = _____

30. 3 + 10 = _____

31. 100 + 75 = _____

32. 100 + 32 = _____

33. 100 + 46 = _____

34. 100 + 37 = _____

35. 100 + 50 = _____

36. 100 + 3 = _____

37. 100 + 9 = _____

38. 200 + 17 = _____

39. 200 + 10 = _____

40. 200 + 1 = _____

41. Hours in a day = _____

42. Days in a week = _____

43. 20 + 40 = _____

44. 30 + 20 = _____

45. 50 + 30 = _____

46. 80 + 10 = _____

47. 20 + 50 = _____

48. 30 + 40 = _____

49. 50 + 40 = _____

50. 20 + 60 = _____

Circle each star as you tally it below.

_____

_____

_____

Practice writing the Chinese
numeral for nine on the lines.

九

_____

_____

My score: _____ My time: _____ min _____ s

The main thing I didn't understand was _____.

I now know that _____

_____

Write the number for each month.

1. March = _____

2. July = _____

3. April = _____

4. August = _____

5. February = _____

6. May = _____

7. November = _____

8. January = _____

9. June = _____

10. December = _____

11. $10 + 3 =$ _____

12. $7 + 5 =$ _____

13. $1 + 12 =$ _____

14. $5 + 6 =$ _____

15. $2 + 8 =$ _____

16. $3 + 10 =$ _____

17. $5 + 7 =$ _____

18. $6 + 5 =$ _____

19. $5 + 5 =$ _____

20. $4 + 9 =$ _____

21. $4 + 3 =$ _____

22. $4 + 6 =$ _____

23. $5 + 8 =$ _____

24. $6 + 4 =$ _____

25. $6 + 7 =$ _____

26. $9 + 4 =$ _____

27. $4 + 7 =$ _____

28. $4 + 8 =$ _____

29. $3 + 8 =$ _____

30. $5 + 3 =$ _____

31. $2 + 11 =$ _____

32. $8 + 4 =$ _____

33. $3 + 7 =$ _____

34. $11 + 2 =$ _____

35. $8 + 5 =$ _____

36. $3 + 6 =$ _____

37. $6 + 6 =$ _____

38. $7 + 4 =$ _____

39. $5 + 4 =$ _____

40. $7 + 6 =$ _____

41. $13 - 7 =$ _____

42. $13 - 6 =$ _____

43. $13 - 4 =$ _____

44. $13 - 12 =$ _____

45. $13 - 5 =$ _____

46. $13 - 8 =$ _____

47. $13 - 10 =$ _____

48. $13 - 9 =$ _____

49. $13 - 3 =$ _____

50. $13 - 11 =$ _____

Practice writing the Chinese numeral for ten on the lines.

_____

_____

Do you know how many? (All answers are different.)

_____ for a touchdown in football?

_____ for a basket in basketball?

_____ for the first point in a tennis game?

My score: _____ My time: _____ min _____ s

The main thing I didn't understand was _____.

I now know that _____

_____.

1. $0 + 13 = $ ____	26. $3 + 2 = $ ____	51. $0 + 13 = $ ____	76. $12 + 1 = $ ____
2. $13 + 0 = $ ____	27. $7 + 3 = $ ____	52. $3 + 7 = $ ____	77. $7 + 6 = $ ____
3. $4 + 5 = $ ____	28. $1 + 9 = $ ____	53. $0 + 12 = $ ____	78. $5 + 7 = $ ____
4. $5 + 4 = $ ____	29. $8 + 2 = $ ____	54. $10 + 3 = $ ____	79. $3 + 8 = $ ____
5. $12 + 1 = $ ____	30. $2 + 8 = $ ____	55. $1 + 11 = $ ____	80. $3 + 7 = $ ____
6. $1 + 12 = $ ____	31. $12 + 1 = $ ____	56. $4 + 9 = $ ____	81. $4 + 9 = $ ____
7. $3 + 5 = $ ____	32. $9 + 1 = $ ____	57. $6 + 6 = $ ____	82. $6 + 3 = $ ____
8. $6 + 7 = $ ____	33. $10 + 0 = $ ____	58. $7 + 5 = $ ____	83. $4 + 7 = $ ____
9. $7 + 6 = $ ____	34. $0 + 9 = $ ____	59. $0 + 13 = $ ____	84. $7 + 4 = $ ____
10. $5 + 3 = $ ____	35. $8 + 5 = $ ____	60. $3 + 10 = $ ____	85. $5 + 5 = $ ____
11. $2 + 11 = $ ____	36. $5 + 8 = $ ____	61. $5 + 6 = $ ____	86. $7 + 6 = $ ____
12. $3 + 4 = $ ____	37. $4 + 6 = $ ____	62. $2 + 10 = $ ____	87. $7 + 4 = $ ____
13. $11 + 2 = $ ____	38. $11 + 2 = $ ____	63. $6 + 7 = $ ____	88. $4 + 7 = $ ____
14. $8 + 5 = $ ____	39. $0 + 10 = $ ____	64. $3 + 9 = $ ____	89. $8 + 4 = $ ____
15. $5 + 8 = $ ____	40. $6 + 7 = $ ____	65. $9 + 4 = $ ____	90. $6 + 7 = $ ____
16. $4 + 3 = $ ____	41. $6 + 4 = $ ____	66. $4 + 8 = $ ____	91. $5 + 6 = $ ____
17. $6 + 7 = $ ____	42. $13 + 0 = $ ____	67. $11 + 2 = $ ____	92. $9 + 4 = $ ____
18. $2 + 4 = $ ____	43. $10 + 3 = $ ____	68. $2 + 11 = $ ____	93. $6 + 5 = $ ____
19. $3 + 10 = $ ____	44. $5 + 5 = $ ____	69. $5 + 7 = $ ____	94. $8 + 5 = $ ____
20. $7 + 6 = $ ____	45. $7 + 6 = $ ____	70. $7 + 5 = $ ____	95. $3 + 7 = $ ____
21. $4 + 2 = $ ____	46. $9 + 4 = $ ____	71. $13 + 0 = $ ____	96. $11 + 2 = $ ____
22. $10 + 3 = $ ____	47. $4 + 9 = $ ____	72. $1 + 12 = $ ____	97. $6 + 4 = $ ____
23. $2 + 3 = $ ____	48. $4 + 8 = $ ____	73. $8 + 5 = $ ____	98. $5 + 8 = $ ____
24. $9 + 4 = $ ____	49. $8 + 4 = $ ____	74. $6 + 6 = $ ____	99. $4 + 6 = $ ____
25. $4 + 9 = $ ____	50. $5 + 5 = $ ____	75. $5 + 8 = $ ____	100. $8 + 3 = $ ____

My score: _____ My time: _____ min _____ s

The main thing I didn't understand was _____.

I now know that _____
_____.

 I'm happy   I'm not happy

Math Speed Tests – Book 1

14 + 0 = 14
13 + 1 = 14
12 + 2 = 14
11 + 3 = 14
10 + 4 = 14
9 + 5 = 14
8 + 6 = 14
7 + 7 = 14
6 + 8 = 14
5 + 9 = 14
4 + 10 = 14
3 + 11 = 14
2 + 12 = 14
1 + 13 = 14
0 + 14 = 14

14 − 0 = 14
14 − 1 = 13
14 − 2 = 12
14 − 3 = 11
14 − 4 = 10
14 − 5 = 9
14 − 6 = 8
14 − 7 = 7
14 − 8 = 6
14 − 9 = 5
14 − 10 = 4
14 − 11 = 3
14 − 12 = 2
14 − 13 = 1
14 − 14 = 0

6 + 8	8 + 6	7 + 7	4 + 10	5 + 9	9 + 5	6 + 8	0 + 11	6 + 5
1 + 10	10 + 1	4 + 5	4 + 7	9 + 4	4 + 6	8 + 6	11 + 0	5 + 6
2 + 12	12 + 2	1 + 13	13 + 1	0 + 14	14 + 0	7 + 7	4 + 7	3 + 2
3 + 11	9 + 2	2 + 9	2 + 10	10 + 2	9 + 3	3 + 9	2 + 5	7 + 4
11 + 3	4 + 10	10 + 4	5 + 9	9 + 5	8 + 6	6 + 8	9 + 5	5 + 9
8 + 3	3 + 8	1 + 11	8 + 2	2 + 8	7 + 3	6 + 6	7 + 5	4 + 10
1 + 13	13 + 1	14 + 0	0 + 12	3 + 7	6 + 4	3 + 11	11 + 3	10 + 4
12 + 2	4 + 7	0 + 14	1 + 13	13 + 1	12 + 2	2 + 12	4 + 8	5 + 7
2 + 12	7 + 4	11 + 1	12 + 0	5 + 5	4 + 6	8 + 4	5 + 6	6 + 5
11 + 3	3 + 11	4 + 10	10 + 4	5 + 9	9 + 5	6 + 8	8 + 6	7 + 7

13 = one baker's dozen

20 = one score

10 = one decade

14 rolling plums

7 fairies = 14 wings

Bruce is going to Jim's place to get some help with his homework.

He is having trouble with addition facts that equal fourteen.

To get him warmed up Jim has left a trail of facts that add to fourteen.

Color the path and you will see the path he takes. You can only travel up, down and across, not diagonally.

My score: _____ My time: _____ min _____ s

The main thing I didn't understand was _____.

I now know that _____

_____.

I'm happy

I'm not happy

OOPS!

I didn't understand

1. $6 + 5 =$ _____

2. $10 + 4 =$ _____

3. $3 + 9 =$ _____

4. $6 + 8 =$ _____

5. $9 + 3 =$ _____

6. $7 + 3 =$ _____

7. $13 + 1 =$ _____

8. $3 + 8 =$ _____

9. $3 + 7 =$ _____

10. $9 + 5 =$ _____

11. $5 + 9 =$ _____

12. $4 + 7 =$ _____

13. $8 + 6 =$ _____

14. $6 + 8 =$ _____

15. $8 + 5 =$ _____

16. $8 + 3 =$ _____

17. $6 + 4 =$ _____

18. $7 + 6 =$ _____

19. $6 + 7 =$ _____

20. $12 + 2 =$ _____

21. $4 + 6 =$ _____

22. $4 + 9 =$ _____

23. $7 + 7 =$ _____

24. $9 + 4 =$ _____

25. $7 + 4 =$ _____

26. $8 + 6 =$ _____

27. $5 + 8 =$ _____

28. $8 + 4 =$ _____

29. $4 + 7 =$ _____

30. $14 + 0 =$ _____

31. $5 + 6 =$ _____

32. $6 + 7 =$ _____

33. $7 + 6 =$ _____

34. $11 + 3 =$ _____

35. $4 + 8 =$ _____

36. $13 - 6 =$ _____

37. $13 - 7 =$ _____

38. $13 - 8 =$ _____

39. $13 - 5 =$ _____

40. $13 - 9 =$ _____

41. $14 - 8 =$ _____

42. $14 - 6 =$ _____

43. $14 - 2 =$ _____

44. $14 - 12 =$ _____

45. $14 - 10 =$ _____

46. $14 - 4 =$ _____

47. $14 - 5 =$ _____

48. $14 - 9 =$ _____

49. $14 - 11 =$ _____

50. $14 - 7 =$ _____

Chinese numerals are written vertically (up and down) rather than horizontally (across). Copy these and see if you can find out how the Chinese system works.

43 = 四十三   57 = 五十七   68 = 六十八   29 = 二十九

My score: _____ My time: _____ min _____ s

The main thing I didn't understand was _____.

I now know that _____

_____

1. 6 + 6 = _____

2. 13 + 1 = _____

3. 8 + 5 = _____

4. 5 + 8 = _____

5. 11 + 3 = _____

6. 5 + 6 = _____

7. 9 + 5 = _____

8. 6 + 5 = _____

9. 7 + 7 = _____

10. 5 + 6 = _____

11. 8 + 6 = _____

12. 6 + 5 = _____

13. 9 + 5 = _____

14. 6 + 8 = _____

15. 5 + 7 = _____

16. 12 + 2 = _____

17. 8 + 4 = _____

18. 10 + 4 = _____

19. 7 + 4 = _____

20. 8 + 6 = _____

21. 4 + 6 = _____

22. 14 + 0 = _____

23. 3 + 7 = _____

24. 8 + 5 = _____

25. 4 + 7 = _____

26. 7 + 7 = _____

27. 8 + 6 = _____

28. 6 + 5 = _____

29. 7 + 5 = _____

30. 13 + 1 = _____

31. 14 – 3 = _____

32. 14 – 11 = _____

33. 14 – 4 = _____

34. 14 – 10 = _____

35. 14 – 5 = _____

36. 14 – 9 = _____

37. 14 – 2 = _____

38. 14 – 7 = _____

39. 14 – 8 = _____

40. 14 – 6 = _____

41. 100 + 1 = _____

42. 100 + 6 = _____

43. 100 + 32 = _____

44. 100 + 51 = _____

45. 100 + 12 = _____

46. 100 + 50 + 7 = _____

47. 100 + 30 + 4 = _____

48. Hours in a day = _____

49. Days in a week = _____

50. Days in a year = _____

Copy these Chinese numerals. Have you figured out the system yet?

41 = 四   65 = 六   72 = 七   98 = 九
      十   十   十   十
      一   五   二   八

My score: _____ My time: _____ min _____ s

The main thing I didn't understand was _____.

I now know that _____

_____.

1.   3 + 4 = _____

2.   9 + 4 = _____

3.   3 + 9 = _____

4.   6 + 8 = _____

5.   3 + 10 = _____

6.   5 + 6 = _____

7.   11 + 3 = _____

8.   6 + 6 = _____

9.   12 + 2 = _____

10.   8 + 5 = _____

11.   5 + 7 = _____

12.   8 + 6 = _____

13.   8 + 4 = _____

14.   6 + 5 = _____

15.   5 + 9 = _____

16.   7 + 5 = _____

17.   3 + 7 = _____

18.   9 + 5 = _____

19.   4 + 8 = _____

20.   4 + 7 = _____

21.   4 + 10 = _____

22.   5 + 8 = _____

23.   2 + 12 = _____

24.   4 + 9 = _____

25.   10 + 4 = _____

26.   3 + 11 = _____

27.   7 + 6 = _____

28.   1 + 13 = _____

29.   6 + 7 = _____

30.   7 + 7 = _____

31.   30 – 1 = _____

32.   10 – 1 = _____

33.   40 – 1 = _____

34.   60 – 1 = _____

35.   100 – 1 = _____

36.   20 – 1 = _____

37.   70 – 1 = _____

38.   90 – 1 = _____

39.   50 – 1 = _____

40.   80 – 1 = _____

41.   100 + 20 + 4 = _____

42.   200 + 40 + 3 = _____

43.   500 + 30 + 7 = _____

44.   800 + 90 + 6 = _____

45.   600 + 50 + 8 = _____

46.   300 + 60 + 5 = _____

47.   400 + 30 + 2 = _____

48.   700 + 80 + 9 = _____

49.   900 + 70 + 3 = _____

50.   400 + 10 + 1 = _____

Design your own bills.

Practice writing the Chinese numeral for ten on the lines.

_____

_____

My score: _____ My time: _____ min _____ s

The main thing I didn't understand was _____.

I now know that _____

_____.

1. 7 + 4 = _____

2. 9 + 5 = _____

3. 11 + 3 = _____

4. 4 + 3 = _____

5. 7 + 6 = _____

6. 2 + 12 = _____

7. 5 + 4 = _____

8. 7 + 5 = _____

9. 9 + 3 = _____

10. 12 + 2 = _____

11. 7 + 7 = _____

12. 4 + 5 = _____

13. 3 + 9 = _____

14. 5 + 6 = _____

15. 5 + 9 = _____

16. 6 + 4 = _____

17. 4 + 10 = _____

18. 6 + 7 = _____

19. 4 + 6 = _____

20. 1 + 13 = _____

21. 3 + 5 = _____

22. 4 + 7 = _____

23. 3 + 11 = _____

24. 6 + 5 = _____

25. 4 + 8 = _____

26. 8 + 6 = _____

27. 8 + 4 = _____

28. 6 + 8 = _____

29. 5 + 7 = _____

30. 3 + 4 = _____

31. 14 – 3 = _____

32. 13 – 6 = _____

33. 14 – 8 = _____

34. 14 – 6 = _____

35. 13 – 7 = _____

36. 13 – 5 = _____

37. 14 – 9 = _____

38. 13 – 4 = _____

39. 13 – 8 = _____

40. 14 – 5 = _____

41. 12 – 8 = _____

42. 14 – 7 = _____

43. 12 – 9 = _____

44. 12 – 5 = _____

45. 14 – 3 = _____

46. Hours in a day = _____

47. Days in a year = _____

48. 60 + 200 + 3 = _____

49. 3 + 70 + 400 = _____

50. 400 + 2 + 90 = _____

Copy these Chinese numerals.

Can you figure out the system for numbers with hundreds in them?

365 =

437 =

892 =

My score: _____ My time: _____ min _____ s

The main thing I didn't understand was _____.

I now know that _____

_____.

1. 1 + 13 = _____	26. 6 + 8 = _____	51. 8 + 6 = _____	76. 4 + 7 = _____
2. 4 + 3 = _____	27. 4 + 4 = _____	52. 3 + 10 = _____	77. 7 + 4 = _____
3. 7 + 7 = _____	28. 7 + 7 = _____	53. 3 + 11 = _____	78. 5 + 7 = _____
4. 3 + 4 = _____	29. 2 + 6 = _____	54. 10 + 3 = _____	79. 7 + 5 = _____
5. 1 + 6 = _____	30. 6 + 2 = _____	55. 11 + 3 = _____	80. 4 + 7 = _____
6. 0 + 14 = _____	31. 14 + 0 = _____	56. 7 + 6 = _____	81. 5 + 6 = _____
7. 6 + 1 = _____	32. 6 + 7 = _____	57. 2 + 11 = _____	82. 5 + 9 = _____
8. 9 + 5 = _____	33. 7 + 6 = _____	58. 4 + 10 = _____	83. 9 + 5 = _____
9. 14 + 0 = _____	34. 9 + 5 = _____	59. 10 + 4 = _____	84. 6 + 5 = _____
10. 5 + 9 = _____	35. 5 + 9 = _____	60. 11 + 2 = _____	85. 8 + 4 = _____
11. 7 + 0 = _____	36. 4 + 9 = _____	61. 6 + 6 = _____	86. 4 + 8 = _____
12. 8 + 6 = _____	37. 1 + 12 = _____	62. 6 + 8 = _____	87. 6 + 5 = _____
13. 10 + 4 = _____	38. 0 + 14 = _____	63. 5 + 9 = _____	88. 5 + 6 = _____
14. 12 + 2 = _____	39. 6 + 8 = _____	64. 3 + 8 = _____	89. 3 + 9 = _____
15. 2 + 5 = _____	40. 8 + 6 = _____	65. 8 + 4 = _____	90. 9 + 3 = _____
16. 11 + 3 = _____	41. 8 + 5 = _____	66. 4 + 8 = _____	91. 10 + 10 = _____
17. 3 + 11 = _____	42. 5 + 8 = _____	67. 8 + 6 = _____	92. A score = _____
18. 5 + 2 = _____	43. 13 + 1 = _____	68. 1 + 1 = _____	93. 20 + 20 = _____
19. 4 + 10 = _____	44. 6 + 7 = _____	69. 9 + 5 = _____	94. 2 score = _____
20. 8 + 6 = _____	45. 1 + 13 = _____	70. 7 + 5 = _____	95. 3 score = _____
21. 13 + 1 = _____	46. 12 + 1 = _____	71. 5 + 7 = _____	96. 23 + 10 = _____
22. 3 + 5 = _____	47. 7 + 7 = _____	72. 6 + 8 = _____	97. 45 + 10 = _____
23. 2 + 12 = _____	48. 9 + 4 = _____	73. 8 + 3 = _____	98. 36 + 10 = _____
24. 5 + 3 = _____	49. 12 + 2 = _____	74. 8 + 6 = _____	99. 15 + 10 = _____
25. 8 + 6 = _____	50. 2 + 12 = _____	75. 6 + 8 = _____	100. 58 + 10 = _____

My score: _____ My time: _____ min _____ s

The main thing I didn't understand was _____.

I now know that _____

_____.

15 + 0 = 15
14 + 1 = 15
13 + 2 = 15
12 + 3 = 15
11 + 4 = 15
10 + 5 = 15
9 + 6 = 15
8 + 7 = 15
7 + 8 = 15
6 + 9 = 15
5 + 10 = 15
4 + 11 = 15
3 + 12 = 15
2 + 13 = 15
1 + 14 = 15
0 + 15 = 15

15 − 0 = 15
15 − 1 = 14
15 − 2 = 13
15 − 3 = 12
15 − 4 = 11
15 − 5 = 10
15 − 6 = 9
15 − 7 = 8

9 + 6	7 + 8	0 + 3	2 + 6	2 + 5	1 + 9	2 + 13	13 + 2	12 + 3
0 + 2	8 + 7	0 + 1	0 + 4	2 + 4	1 + 7	14 + 1	0 + 5	3 + 12
1 + 6	4 + 11	11 + 4	6 + 9	9 + 6	0 + 6	1 + 14	1 + 8	11 + 4
2 + 7	2 + 12	2 + 10	0 + 11	7 + 8	2 + 3	0 + 15	1 + 2	4 + 11
0 + 9	3 + 3	2 + 11	9 + 6	8 + 7	0 + 8	15 + 0	0 + 7	5 + 10
2 + 8	3 + 7	0 + 10	6 + 9	1 + 11	1 + 10	8 + 7	1 + 3	10 + 5
2 + 9	4 + 1	3 + 4	10 + 5	1 + 4	1 + 1	7 + 8	1 + 12	6 + 9
3 + 2	4 + 3	3 + 8	5 + 10	2 + 0	10 + 5	9 + 6	0 + 14	9 + 6
3 + 6	4 + 6	3 + 10	11 + 4	4 + 11	5 + 10	0 + 13	1 + 13	8 + 7
3 + 11	3 + 9	3 + 5	3 + 1	2 + 2	2 + 1	1 + 5	0 + 12	7 + 8

15 − 6 = 9
15 − 7 = 8

15 − 8 = 7
15 − 9 = 6
15 − 10 = 5
15 − 11 = 4
15 − 12 = 3
15 − 13 = 2
15 − 14 = 1
15 − 15 = 0

15 grubs on the way to the football game.

Where Jim lives they have $3 bills. Five of these make $15.

Jim loves to chomp on chop suey. He buys it at the Cheerful Cheap Chop Suey Store.
He always goes the same way.

Color the path he takes by coloring all the squares that add to fifteen. You can only travel up, down and across, not diagonally.

Five runners in a three-legged race = 15 legs

My score: _____ My time: _____ min _____ s

The main thing I didn't understand was _____.

I now know that _____

_____.

Facts Tested: + to 15 and hundreds + tens + ones

1. 4 + 6 = _____

2. 7 + 7 = _____

3. 2 + 13 = _____

4. 9 + 5 = _____

5. 7 + 5 = _____

6. 3 + 12 = _____

7. 5 + 9 = _____

8. 12 + 3 = _____

9. 13 + 2 = _____

10. 6 + 5 = _____

11. 4 + 11 = _____

12. 10 + 4 = _____

13. 5 + 6 = _____

14. 6 + 9 = _____

15. 7 + 4 = _____

16. 5 + 2 = _____

17. 4 + 5 = _____

18. 7 + 8 = _____

19. 8 + 7 = _____

20. 6 + 8 = _____

21. 3 + 5 = _____

22. 0 + 15 = _____

23. 5 + 4 = _____

24. 14 + 1 = _____

25. 3 + 8 = _____

26. 5 + 10 = _____

27. 7 + 8 = _____

28. 7 + 6 = _____

29. 4 + 7 = _____

30. 11 + 4 = _____

31. 9 + 6 = _____

32. 5 + 8 = _____

33. 8 + 3 = _____

34. 1 + 14 = _____

35. 4 + 3 = _____

36. 8 + 5 = _____

37. 10 + 5 = _____

38. 8 + 6 = _____

39. 6 + 7 = _____

40. 8 + 7 = _____

41. 100 + 30 + 7 = _____

42. 600 + 70 + 4 = _____

43. 500 + 60 + 1 = _____

44. 700 + 30 + 8 = _____

45. 200 + 70 + 3 = _____

46. 400 + 70 + 6 = _____

47. 900 + 40 + 3 = _____

48. 300 + 60 + 5 = _____

49. 800 + 90 + 7 = _____

50. 200 + 40 + 5 = _____

Copy these Chinese numerals. Write some of your own.

145 = 一百四十五

____ ____ = ____

____ = ____

My score: _____ My time: _____ min _____ s

The main thing I didn't understand was _____.

I now know that _____

_____.

1. $4 + 9 =$ _____
2. $10 + 5 =$ _____
3. $8 + 4 =$ _____
4. $6 + 5 =$ _____
5. $9 + 6 =$ _____
6. $6 + 9 =$ _____
7. $4 + 8 =$ _____
8. $3 + 12 =$ _____
9. $5 + 6 =$ _____
10. $7 + 8 =$ _____
11. $7 + 4 =$ _____
12. $8 + 7 =$ _____
13. $4 + 6 =$ _____
14. $3 + 8 =$ _____
15. $13 + 2 =$ _____
16. $12 + 3 =$ _____
17. $5 + 9 =$ _____

18. $9 + 4 =$ _____
19. $11 + 4 =$ _____
20. $7 + 5 =$ _____
21. $5 + 3 =$ _____
22. $8 + 7 =$ _____
23. $7 + 8 =$ _____
24. $4 + 7 =$ _____
25. $6 + 7 =$ _____
26. $7 + 6 =$ _____
27. $4 + 11 =$ _____
28. $4 + 5 =$ _____
29. $14 + 1 =$ _____
30. $3 + 7 =$ _____
31. $9 + 5 =$ _____
32. $5 + 7 =$ _____
33. $7 + 3 =$ _____
34. $5 + 10 =$ _____

35. $8 + 5 =$ _____
36. $5 + 8 =$ _____
37. $6 + 4 =$ _____
38. $15 + 0 =$ _____
39. $6 + 8 =$ _____
40. $8 + 6 =$ _____
41. $15 - 1 =$ _____
42. $15 - 8 =$ _____
43. $15 - 5 =$ _____
44. $15 - 7 =$ _____
45. $15 - 2 =$ _____
46. $15 - 10 =$ _____
47. $15 - 4 =$ _____
48. $15 - 6 =$ _____
49. $15 - 9 =$ _____
50. $15 - 3 =$ _____

Do you know how many singers in a:

duo? _____   trio? _____

quartet? _____   quintet? _____

sextet? _____

Design some coins below.

My score: _____ My time: _____ min _____ s

The main thing I didn't understand was _____.

I now know that _____

_____.

1.　3 + 12 = _____

2.　5 + 9 = _____

3.　4 + 7 = _____

4.　6 + 9 = _____

5.　7 + 7 = _____

6.　6 + 7 = _____

7.　8 + 7 = _____

8.　7 + 8 = _____

9.　5 + 7 = _____

10.　4 + 11 = _____

11.　7 + 5 = _____

12.　9 + 6 = _____

13.　7 + 7 = _____

14.　1 + 14 = _____

15.　6 + 8 = _____

16.　5 + 8 = _____

17.　3 + 7 = _____

18.　5 + 10 = _____

19.　8 + 7 = _____

20.　4 + 3 = _____

21.　6 + 4 = _____

22.　10 + 5 = _____

23.　12 + 3 = _____

24.　8 + 5 = _____

25.　11 + 4 = _____

26.　6 + 5 = _____

27.　13 + 2 = _____

28.　8 + 6 = _____

29.　7 + 6 = _____

30.　7 + 8 = _____

31.　15 – 7 = _____

32.　25 – 7 = _____

33.　35 – 7 = _____

34.　45 – 7 = _____

35.　55 – 7 = _____

36.　65 – 7 = _____

37.　75 – 7 = _____

38.　85 – 7 = _____

39.　95 – 7 = _____

40.　105 – 7 = _____

41.　10 – 3 = _____

42.　20 – 3 = _____

43.　30 – 3 = _____

44.　40 – 3 = _____

45.　50 – 3 = _____

46.　60 – 3 = _____

47.　70 – 3 = _____

48.　80 – 3 = _____

49.　90 – 3 = _____

50.　100 – 3 = _____

Measure the lines in centimeters. Write their length in the space provided.

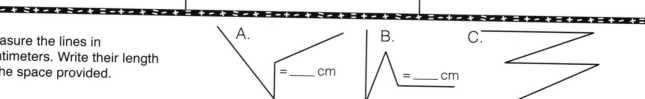

A.　= ____ cm

B.　= ____ cm

C.　= ____ cm

My score: _____　My time: _____ min _____ s

The main thing I didn't understand was _____.

I now know that _____

_____

I'm happy　　I'm not happy　　OOPS!　　I didn't understand

1.   5 + 8 = _____

2.   7 + 6 = _____

3.   4 + 9 = _____

4.   12 + 3 = _____

5.   6 + 6 = _____

6.   7 + 8 = _____

7.   6 + 5 = _____

8.   8 + 7 = _____

9.   7 + 5 = _____

10. 3 + 6 = _____

11. 9 + 6 = _____

12. 2 + 13 = _____

13. 3 + 12 = _____

14. 7 + 4 = _____

15. 6 + 9 = _____

16. 7 + 3 = _____

17. 5 + 10 = _____

18. 10 + 5 = _____

19. 9 + 4 = _____

20. 2 + 8 = _____

21. 4 + 11 = _____

22. 7 + 2 = _____

23. 4 + 5 = _____

24. 11 + 4 = _____

25. 7 + 1 = _____

26. 4 + 8 = _____

27. 8 + 5 = _____

28. 8 + 7 = _____

29. 3 + 5 = _____

30. 7 + 7 = _____

31. 13 – 7 = _____

32. 13 – 6 = _____

33. 15 – 7 = _____

34. 15 – 8 = _____

35. 15 – 4 = _____

36. 14 – 8 = _____

37. 14 – 6 = _____

38. 12 – 7 = _____

39. 11 – 6 = _____

40. 10 – 8 = _____

41. 9 + 4 = _____

42. 19 + 4 = _____

43. 29 + 4 = _____

44. 39 + 4 = _____

45. 49 + 4 = _____

46. 59 + 4 = _____

47. 69 + 4 = _____

48. 79 + 4 = _____

49. 89 + 4 = _____

50. 99 + 4 = _____

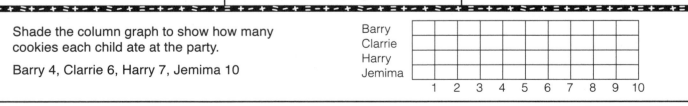

Shade the column graph to show how many cookies each child ate at the party.

Barry 4, Clarrie 6, Harry 7, Jemima 10

	1	2	3	4	5	6	7	8	9	10
Barry										
Clarrie										
Harry										
Jemima										

My score: _____ My time: _____ min _____ s

The main thing I didn't understand was _____.

I now know that _____

_____.

I'm happy   I'm not happy   OOPS!   I didn't understand

1. 5 + 9 = _____	26. 65 – 3 = _____	51. 11 – 2 = _____	76. 4 + 11 = _____
2. 11 + 4 = _____	27. 75 – 3 = _____	52. 21 – 2 = _____	77. 8 + 3 = _____
3. 1 + 11 = _____	28. 85 – 3 = _____	53. 31 – 2 = _____	78. 14 + 0 = _____
4. 8 + 7 = _____	29. 95 – 3 = _____	54. 41 – 2 = _____	79. 7 + 4 = _____
5. 5 + 7 = _____	30. 105 – 3 = _____	55. 51 – 2 = _____	80. 0 + 15 = _____
6. 15 + 0 = _____	31. 12 + 3 = _____	56. 61 – 2 = _____	81. 8 + 7 = _____
7. 2 + 11 = _____	32. 6 + 8 = _____	57. 71 – 2 = _____	82. 18 + 7 = _____
8. 2 + 10 = _____	33. 3 + 10 = _____	58. 81 – 2 = _____	83. 28 + 7 = _____
9. 6 + 9 = _____	34. 7 + 8 = _____	59. 91 – 2 = _____	84. 38 + 7 = _____
10. 9 + 6 = _____	35. 6 + 5 = _____	60. 101 – 2 = _____	85. 48 + 7 = _____
11. 5 + 8 = _____	36. 4 + 10 = _____	61. 8 + 5 = _____	86. 58 + 7 = _____
12. 7 + 8 = _____	37. 3 + 9 = _____	62. 3 + 8 = _____	87. 68 + 7 = _____
13. 7 + 5 = _____	38. 14 + 1 = _____	63. 3 + 12 = _____	88. 78 + 7 = _____
14. 8 + 6 = _____	39. 4 + 8 = _____	64. 3 + 7 = _____	89. 88 + 7 = _____
15. 13 + 2 = _____	40. 2 + 12 = _____	65. 3 + 11 = _____	90. 98 + 7 = _____
16. 6 + 6 = _____	41. 6 + 7 = _____	66. 8 + 7 = _____	91. 20 + 20 = _____
17. 9 + 4 = _____	42. 7 + 6 = _____	67. 7 + 8 = _____	92. 20 + 30 = _____
18. 10 + 5 = _____	43. 2 + 13 = _____	68. 9 + 5 = _____	93. 30 + 30 = _____
19. 5 + 6 = _____	44. 8 + 4 = _____	69. 4 + 7 = _____	94. 40 + 30 = _____
20. 13 + 0 = _____	45. 8 + 7 = _____	70. 6 + 4 = _____	95. 20 + 70 = _____
21. 15 – 3 = _____	46. 6 + 5 = _____	71. 1 + 14 = _____	96. 65 + 10 = _____
22. 25 – 3 = _____	47. 5 + 10 = _____	72. 4 + 9 = _____	97. 42 + 10 = _____
23. 35 – 3 = _____	48. 5 + 7 = _____	73. 7 + 7 = _____	98. 27 + 10 = _____
24. 45 – 3 = _____	49. 9 + 3 = _____	74. 1 + 12 = _____	99. 68 + 10 = _____
25. 55 – 3 = _____	50. 1 + 13 = _____	75. 4 + 6 = _____	100. 39 + 10 = _____

My score: _____　My time: _____ min _____ s

The main thing I didn't understand was _____.

I now know that _____
_____.

7 + 9	9 + 7	8 + 8	13 + 3	12 + 4	11 + 5	5 + 11	6 + 10	10 + 6
6 + 4	8 + 6	5 + 4	8 + 5	8 + 6	6 + 3	4 + 6	8 + 4	8 + 8
5 + 11	11 + 5	10 + 6	6 + 10	7 + 9	9 + 7	8 + 8	7 + 9	9 + 7
4 + 12	8 + 5	5 + 6	6 + 5	9 + 1	3 + 6	7 + 3	1 + 8	4 + 8
12 + 4	13 + 3	4 + 5	7 + 2	1 + 9	3 + 7	3 + 11	3 + 7	2 + 5
8 + 4	3 + 13	6 + 8	1 + 15	2 + 14	14 + 2	13 + 3	3 + 13	4 + 12
8 + 7	2 + 14	8 + 6	15 + 1	8 + 2	2 + 8	5 + 9	9 + 5	12 + 4
7 + 6	14 + 2	7 + 7	16 + 0	7 + 8	4 + 6	6 + 10	5 + 11	11 + 5
6 + 7	15 + 1	1 + 15	0 + 16	4 + 4	3 + 2	10 + 6	7 + 6	6 + 7
7 + 8	3 + 5	10 + 4	8 + 7	2 + 5	1 + 1	7 + 9	9 + 7	8 + 8

16 + 0 = 16
15 + 1 = 16
14 + 2 = 16
13 + 3 = 16
12 + 4 = 16
11 + 5 = 16
10 + 6 = 16
9 + 7 = 16
8 + 8 = 16
7 + 9 = 16
6 + 10 = 16
5 + 11 = 16
4 + 12 = 16
3 + 13 = 16
2 + 14 = 16
1 + 15 = 16
0 + 16 = 16

16 − 0 = 16
16 − 1 = 15
16 − 2 = 14
16 − 3 = 13
16 − 4 = 12
16 − 5 = 11
16 − 6 = 10
16 − 7 = 9
16 − 8 = 8
16 − 9 = 7
16 − 10 = 6
16 − 11 = 5
16 − 12 = 4
16 − 13 = 3
16 − 14 = 2
16 − 15 = 1
16 − 16 = 0

Help Bruce find his way through the Amazing Mirror Maze House. He has been walking around in circles for hours.

Color the number facts that equal sixteen. This will show him the secret way out. You can only travel up, down and across, not diagonally.

My score: _____ My time: _____ min _____ s

The main thing I didn't understand was _____.

I now know that _____

_____.

I'm happy   I'm not happy

OOPS!   I didn't understand

1. 4 + 9 = _____
2. 3 + 13 = _____
3. 3 + 8 = _____
4. 8 + 8 = _____
5. 8 + 6 = _____
6. 7 + 5 = _____
7. 10 + 6 = _____
8. 7 + 7 = _____
9. 4 + 7 = _____
10. 6 + 10 = _____
11. 6 + 7 = _____
12. 5 + 11 = _____
13. 7 + 6 = _____
14. 8 + 7 = _____
15. 7 + 8 = _____
16. 5 + 6 = _____
17. 9 + 6 = _____

18. 7 + 5 = _____
19. 7 + 9 = _____
20. 6 + 8 = _____
21. 9 + 7 = _____
22. 13 + 3 = _____
23. 8 + 4 = _____
24. 14 + 2 = _____
25. 4 + 8 = _____
26. 2 + 11 = _____
27. 5 + 9 = _____
28. 5 + 10 = _____
29. 6 + 6 = _____
30. 11 + 5 = _____
31. 3 + 7 = _____
32. 6 + 5 = _____
33. 1 + 15 = _____
34. 6 + 9 = _____

35. 5 + 8 = _____
36. 12 + 4 = _____
37. 8 + 5 = _____
38. 5 + 7 = _____
39. 8 + 7 = _____
40. 4 + 12 = _____
41. 100 + 57 = _____
42. 99 + 57 = _____
43. 100 + 63 = _____
44. 99 + 63 = _____
45. 100 + 85 = _____
46. 99 + 85 = _____
47. 100 + 26 = _____
48. 99 + 26 = _____
49. 100 + 74 = _____
50. 99 + 74 = _____

"Quad" in front of a word usually means four.

Butch is a quadruped. He has four legs.

Circle the quadrupeds.

horse   chicken   flea

spider   cow   elephant

boy   shark   snake

Tip

Adding 9 is easy. Just add 10 then take away 1!

37 + 9 = 47 – 1 = 46

My score: _____   My time: _____ min _____ s

The main thing I didn't understand was _____.

I now know that _____

_____

1.　7 + 6 = _____

2.　9 + 7 = _____

3.　8 + 8 = _____

4.　7 + 7 = _____

5.　4 + 7 = _____

6.　2 + 4 = _____

7.　2 + 14 = _____

8.　7 + 9 = _____

9.　5 + 11 = _____

10.　3 + 7 = _____

11.　4 + 8 = _____

12.　12 + 4 = _____

13.　5 + 8 = _____

14.　4 + 12 = _____

15.　6 + 6 = _____

16.　5 + 7 = _____

17.　6 + 8 = _____

18.　9 + 7 = _____

19.　5 + 6 = _____

20.　3 + 6 = _____

21.　6 + 7 = _____

22.　10 + 6 = _____

23.　4 + 6 = _____

24.　7 + 9 = _____

25.　2 + 7 = _____

26.　11 + 5 = _____

27.　8 + 7 = _____

28.　7 + 6 = _____

29.　6 + 10 = _____

30.　7 + 8 = _____

31.　16 minus 10 = _____

32.　16 minus 4 = _____

33.　16 minus 7 = _____

34.　16 minus 12 = _____

35.　16 minus 8 = _____

36.　16 minus 11 = _____

37.　16 minus 9 = _____

38.　16 minus 3 = _____

39.　16 minus 6 = _____

40.　16 minus 5 = _____

41.　99 + 3 = _____

42.　99 + 5 = _____

43.　99 + 7 = _____

44.　99 + 2 = _____

45.　99 + 4 = _____

46.　99 + 45 = _____

47.　99 + 67 = _____

48.　99 + 83 = _____

49.　99 + 26 = _____

50.　99 + 58 = _____

What number am I?

- I'm more than ten and less than twenty.
- I'm an odd number.
- Two of me is less than thirty.
- I'm more than a dozen.

Cross off the numbers below from the clues.
The number left over is the answer.

5	6	7	8	9	
10	11	12	13	14	
15	16	17	18	19	20

My score: _____　My time: _____ min _____ s

The main thing I didn't understand was _____.

I now know that _____

_____.

1. 6 + 9 = _____

2. 3 + 13 = _____

3. 2 + 7 = _____

4. 1 + 15 = _____

5. 13 + 3 = _____

6. 9 + 6 = _____

7. 15 + 1 = _____

8. 8 + 6 = _____

9. 12 + 4 = _____

10. 6 + 8 = _____

11. 4 + 12 = _____

12. 7 + 7 = _____

13. 0 + 16 = _____

14. 5 + 11 = _____

15. 6 + 7 = _____

16. 4 + 8 = _____

17. 8 + 8 = _____

18. 7 + 9 = _____

19. 7 + 6 = _____

20. 9 + 7 = _____

21. 5 + 8 = _____

22. 10 + 6 = _____

23. 6 + 10 = _____

24. 8 + 5 = _____

25. 11 + 5 = _____

26. 4 + 7 = _____

27. 7 + 8 = _____

28. 2 + 14 = _____

29. 8 + 7 = _____

30. 14 + 2 = _____

31. 16 take away 6 = _____

32. 16 take away 5 = _____

33. 16 take away 7 = _____

34. 16 take away 4 = _____

35. 16 take away 8 = _____

36. 14 take away 10 = ___

37. 14 take away 12 = ___

38. 14 take away 1 = ___

39. 14 take away 13 = ___

40. 14 take away 9 = _____

41. 6 tens + 3 ones = _____

42. 4 tens + 2 ones = _____

43. 9 tens + 5 ones = _____

44. 8 tens + 4 ones = _____

45. 7 tens + 6 ones = _____

46. 5 tens + 8 ones = _____

47. 3 tens + 7 ones = _____

48. 1 ten + 9 ones = _____

49. 2 tens + 1 one = _____

50. 6 tens + 5 ones = _____

Read the tally. Shade the graph of favorite toys in the class.

Yo-yo ||| Games |||| ||||

Dolls |||| ||| Ball ||||| |||| Cars |

Yo-yo							
Games							
Dolls							
Ball							
Cars							

My score: _____ My time: _____ min _____ s

The main thing I didn't understand was _____.

I now know that _____
_____

1.   8 + 6 = _____

2.   6 + 4 = _____

3.   8 + 7 = _____

4.   7 + 5 = _____

5.   12 + 4 = _____

6.   8 + 8 = _____

7.   6 + 7 = _____

8.   7 + 8 = _____

9.   5 + 7 = _____

10. 3 + 6 = _____

11. 9 + 7 = _____

12. 6 + 8 = _____

13. 5 + 6 = _____

14. 7 + 9 = _____

15. 5 + 8 = _____

16. 2 + 7 = _____

17. 5 + 11 = _____

18. 6 + 4 = _____

19. 11 + 5 = _____

20. 5 + 6 = _____

21. 14 – 3 = _____

22. 15 – 5 = _____

23. 13 – 6 = _____

24. 12 – 4 = _____

25. 11 – 8 = _____

26. 14 – 5 = _____

27. 13 – 8 = _____

28. 12 – 0 = _____

29. 13 – 5 = _____

30. 13 – 7 = _____

31. 14 – 6 = _____

32. 11 – 7 = _____

33. 16 – 6 = _____

34. 14 – 7 = _____

35. 16 – 11 = _____

36. 12 – 6 = _____

37. 16 – 9 = _____

38. 10 – 5 = _____

39. 16 – 8 = _____

40. 10 – 7 = _____

41. 100 – 1 = _____

42. 200 – 1 = _____

43. 300 – 1 = _____

44. 400 – 1 = _____

45. 500 – 1 = _____

46. 30 + 40 = _____

47. 20 + 70 = _____

48. 50 + 30 = _____

49. 30 + 20 = _____

50. 40 + 50 = _____

Poor Jim is lost. Help him through the maze by following only the even numbers. Shade the path so Jim can get to his cottage. The odd squares are full of prickles!

→	2	4	3	17	21	27	31	35	39	48	62	10	→
	1	8	5	30	10	16	100	20	33	64	41	51	
	15	6	11	16	7	19	29	36	37	50	49	45	
	3	12	22	40	9	23	25	44	68	72	43	47	

My score: _____ My time: _____ min _____ s

 I'm happy I'm not happy

The main thing I didn't understand was _____.

I now know that _____

_____.

 OOPS! I didn't understand

1. 11 + 4 = _____
2. 6 + 7 = _____
3. 8 + 7 = _____
4. 7 + 8 = _____
5. 4 + 7 = _____
6. 1 + 15 = _____
7. 10 + 5 = _____
8. 7 + 7 = _____
9. 10 + 6 = _____
10. 0 + 15 = _____
11. 8 + 6 = _____
12. 6 + 8 = _____
13. 5 + 11 = _____
14. 4 + 8 = _____
15. 7 + 9 = _____
16. 9 + 7 = _____
17. 3 + 12 = _____
18. 9 + 4 = _____
19. 12 + 4 = _____
20. 4 + 5 = _____
21. 6 – 4 = _____
22. 16 – 4 = _____
23. 26 – 4 = _____
24. 36 – 4 = _____
25. 46 – 4 = _____

26. 56 – 4 = _____
27. 66 – 4 = _____
28. 76 – 4 = _____
29. 86 – 4 = _____
30. 96 – 4 = _____
31. 7 + 3 = _____
32. 9 + 6 = _____
33. 5 + 8 = _____
34. 15 + 1 = _____
35. 7 + 4 = _____
36. 6 + 10 = _____
37. 6 + 5 = _____
38. 2 + 14 = _____
39. 6 + 8 = _____
40. 8 + 8 = _____
41. 5 + 9 = _____
42. 16 + 0 = _____
43. 8 + 4 = _____
44. 3 + 13 = _____
45. 5 + 7 = _____
46. 4 + 12 = _____
47. 6 + 4 = _____
48. 4 + 11 = _____
49. 5 + 4 = _____
50. 9 + 7 = _____

51. 16 – 8 = _____
52. 26 – 8 = _____
53. 36 – 8 = _____
54. 46 – 8 = _____
55. 56 – 8 = _____
56. 66 – 8 = _____
57. 76 – 8 = _____
58. 86 – 8 = _____
59. 96 – 8 = _____
60. 106 – 8 = _____
61. 8 + 5 = _____
62. 5 + 6 = _____
63. 7 + 9 = _____
64. 6 + 9 = _____
65. 3 + 7 = _____
66. 3 + 4 = _____
67. 14 + 2 = _____
68. 4 + 6 = _____
69. 5 + 10 = _____
70. 8 + 6 = _____
71. 7 + 6 = _____
72. 13 + 3 = _____
73. 8 + 8 = _____
74. 7 + 5 = _____
75. 5 + 3 = _____

76. 11 + 5 = _____
77. 4 + 9 = _____
78. 4 + 4 = _____
79. 3 + 6 = _____
80. 0 + 16 = _____
81. 40 + 30 = _____
82. 50 + 40 = _____
83. 20 + 30 = _____
84. 50 + 50 = _____
85. 40 + 20 = _____
86. 60 + 30 = _____
87. 20 + 70 = _____
88. 10 + 30 = _____
89. 40 + 40 = _____
90. 20 + 60 = _____
91. 10 + _____ = 16
92. 6 + _____ = 16
93. 2 + _____ = 16
94. 14 + _____ = 16
95. 8 + _____ = 16
96. 3 + _____ = 16
97. 13 + _____ = 16
98. 5 + _____ = 16
99. 9 + _____ = 16
100. 1 + _____ = 16

My score: _____ My time: _____ min _____ s

The main thing I didn't understand was _____.

I now know that _____
_____.

17 + 0	2 + 15	14 + 3	10 + 7	8 + 9	9 + 8	10 + 7	7 + 5	6 + 7
8 + 7	4 + 7	8 + 4	9 + 3	8 + 4	4 + 8	6 + 11	5 + 7	5 + 7
8 + 7	1 + 7	2 + 7	3 + 9	7 + 10	9 + 8	8 + 9	6 + 6	10 + 3
4 + 13	13 + 4	8 + 9	9 + 8	10 + 7	7 + 7	6 + 5	4 + 7	9 + 3
5 + 12	11 + 1	2 + 10	6 + 4	7 + 8	0 + 7	3 + 7	7 + 6	3 + 10
12 + 5	13 + 4	4 + 13	5 + 12	12 + 5	11 + 6	6 + 11	7 + 10	10 + 7
1 + 11	10 + 2	4 + 6	1 + 5	14 + 1	3 + 7	8 + 5	6 + 7	9 + 8
3 + 14	14 + 3	15 + 2	2 + 15	1 + 16	16 + 1	17 + 0	0 + 17	8 + 9
4 + 13	12 + 0	5 + 8	3 + 6	4 + 7	5 + 5	7 + 4	6 + 3	8 + 5
13 + 4	12 + 5	5 + 12	11 + 6	6 + 11	7 + 10	10 + 7	8 + 9	9 + 8

17 + 0 = 17
16 + 1 = 17
15 + 2 = 17
14 + 3 = 17
13 + 4 = 17
12 + 5 = 17
11 + 6 = 17
10 + 7 = 17
9 + 8 = 17
8 + 9 = 17
7 + 10 = 17
6 + 11 = 17
5 + 12 = 17
4 + 13 = 17
3 + 14 = 17
2 + 15 = 17
1 + 16 = 17
0 + 17 = 17

17 − 0 = 17
17 − 1 = 16
17 − 2 = 15
17 − 3 = 14
17 − 4 = 13
17 − 5 = 12
17 − 6 = 11
17 − 7 = 10
17 − 8 = 9   17 − 13 = 4
17 − 9 = 8   17 − 14 = 3
17 − 10 = 7   17 − 15 = 2
17 − 11 = 6   17 − 16 = 1
17 − 12 = 5   17 − 17 = 0

Decorate 17 in an interesting way.

Bruce, thinking about life after he gets to 17.

Jim is running late for football training.

The coach told him he must step on all the squares that add up to seventeen on the big concrete area outside the ground on which he trains. Make it easier for him by coloring them.

You can only travel up, down and across, not diagonally.

My score: _____ My time: _____ min _____ s

The main thing I didn't understand was _____.

I now know that _____

1. 10 and 7 = _____

2. 5 and 12 = _____

3. 6 and 10 = _____

4. 7 and 7 = _____

5. 12 and 5 = _____

6. 9 and 6 = _____

7. 6 and 4 = _____

8. 8 and 9 = _____

9. 9 and 5 = _____

10. 7 and 10 = _____

11. 12 and 4 = _____

12. 5 and 7 = _____

13. 10 and 6 = _____

14. 8 and 4 = _____

15. 10 and 7 = _____

16. 8 and 8 = _____

17. 12 and 3 = _____

18. 11 and 6 = _____

19. 6 and 9 = _____

20. 10 and 5 = _____

21. 7 and 9 = _____

22. 8 and 6 = _____

23. 13 and 4 = _____

24. 4 and 12 = _____

25. 5 and 6 = _____

26. 11 and 5 = _____

27. 7 and 5 = _____

28. 4 and 13 = _____

29. 5 and 8 = _____

30. 4 and 11 = _____

31. 9 and 7 = _____

32. 4 and 7 = _____

33. 6 and 8 = _____

34. 6 and 11 = _____

35. 11 and 4 = _____

36. 3 and 14 = _____

37. 8 and 7 = _____

38. 5 and 11 = _____

39. 7 and 8 = _____

40. 9 and 8 = _____

How many dimes (10¢ coins)?

41. 60¢ = _____

42. 40¢ = _____

43. $1.00 = _____

44. 30¢ = _____

45. 20¢ = _____

46. 50¢ = _____

47. 10¢ = _____

48. 70¢ = _____

49. 90¢ = _____

50. 80¢ = _____

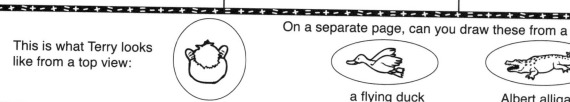

This is what Terry looks like from a top view:

On a separate page, can you draw these from a top view?

a flying duck   Albert alligator

My score: _____ My time: _____ min _____ s

The main thing I didn't understand was _____.

I now know that _____

_____.

 I'm happy   I'm not happy

 OOPS!   I didn't understand

    Math Speed Tests – Book 1

1. 8 plus 8 = _____

2. 9 plus 6 = _____

3. 3 plus 14 = _____

4. 5 plus 9 = _____

5. 7 plus 6 = _____

6. 9 plus 8 = _____

7. 7 plus 7 = _____

8. 7 plus 9 = _____

9. 5 plus 7 = _____

10. 6 plus 11 = _____

11. 10 plus 6 = _____

12. 7 plus 5 = _____

13. 10 plus 7 = _____

14. 8 plus 7 = _____

15. 5 plus 8 = _____

16. 9 plus 7 = _____

17. 7 plus 8 = _____

18. 4 plus 13 = _____

19. 8 plus 6 = _____

20. 12 plus 5 = _____

21. 6 plus 9 = _____

22. 7 plus 10 = _____

23. 6 plus 7 = _____

24. 8 plus 4 = _____

25. 6 plus 10 = _____

26. 11 plus 6 = _____

27. 14 plus 3 = _____

28. 8 plus 5 = _____

29. 5 plus 6 = _____

30. 8 plus 9 = _____

31. 4 plus 7 = _____

32. 11 plus 5 = _____

33. 6 plus 8 = _____

34. 5 plus 12 = _____

35. 9 plus 5 = _____

36. 13 plus 4 = _____

37. 4 plus 8 = _____

38. 5 plus 10 = _____

39. 6 plus 6 = _____

40. 0 plus 17 = _____

41. 17 – 8 = _____

42. 17 – 9 = _____

43. 17 – 7 = _____

44. 17 – 0 = _____

45. 17 – 5 = _____

46. 17 – 14 = _____

47. 17 – 3 = _____

48. 17 – 1 = _____

49. 17 – 6 = _____

50. 17 – 10 = _____

Bruce's wardrobe contains one of each below:

How many combinations can he dress in? _____
List them on a separate piece of paper.

My score: _____ My time: _____ min _____ s

The main thing I didn't understand was _____.

I now know that _____

_____.

1. 8 + 9 = _____

2. 7 + 6 = _____

3. 7 + 5 = _____

4. 4 + 6 = _____

5. 10 + 7 = _____

6. 5 + 7 = _____

7. 11 + 6 = _____

8. 6 + 7 = _____

9. 5 + 4 = _____

10. 14 + 3 = _____

11. 3 + 7 = _____

12. 4 + 5 = _____

13. 13 + 4 = _____

14. 5 + 8 = _____

15. 5 + 6 = _____

16. 6 + 4 = _____

17. 9 + 8 = _____

18. 8 + 5 = _____

19. 6 + 11 = _____

20. 4 + 8 = _____

21. 3 + 4 + 1 = _____

22. 2 + 3 + 5 = _____

23. 4 + 2 + 6 = _____

24. 7 + 3 + 7 = _____

25. 5 + 5 + 6 = _____

26. 4 + 5 + 6 = _____

27. 6 + 6 + 5 = _____

28. 9 + 1 + 5 = _____

29. 4 + 3 + 7 = _____

30. 6 + 3 + 4 = _____

31. 17 – 4 = _____

32. 15 – 5 = _____

33. 17 – 5 = _____

34. 12 – 5 = _____

35. 13 – 7 = _____

36. 14 – 11 = _____

37. 17 – 10 = _____

38. 15 – 7 = _____

39. 17 – 11 = _____

40. 15 – 10 = _____

41. 17 – 6 = _____

42. 17 – 9 = _____

43. 14 – 4 = _____

44. 16 – 8 = _____

45. 17 – 7 = _____

46. 16 – 10 = _____

47. 17 – 16 = _____

48. 14 – 10 = _____

49. 17 – 8 = _____

50. 14 – 3 = _____

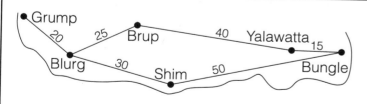

The road map shows the distance between the towns in kilometers. How far is:

Grump to Shim? _____

Blurg to Yalawatta? _____

Grump to Yalawatta? _____

My score: _____ My time: _____ min _____ s

The main thing I didn't understand was _____.

I now know that _____
_____.

Math Speed Tests – Book 1   • 57 •

1.   7 more than 8 = _____

2.   5 more than 11 = _____

3.   2 more than 15 = _____

4.   6 more than 7 = _____

5.   9 more than 5 = _____

6.   5 more than 12 = _____

7.   8 more than 8 = _____

8.   10 more than 7 = _____

9.   13 more than 4 = _____

10. 9 more than 8 = _____

11. 2 more than 11 = _____

12. 1 more than 13 = _____

13. 12 more than 5 = _____

14. 14 more than 3 = _____

15. 16 more than 1= _____

16. 6 more than 11 = _____

17. 7 more than 8 = _____

18. 5 more than 6 = _____

19. 15 more than 2 = _____

20. 11 more than 6 = _____

21. 4 more than 11 = _____

22. 9 more than 6 = _____

23. 10 more than 3 = _____

24. 8 more than 6 = _____

25. 3 more than 14 = _____

26. 8 more than 9 = _____

27. 7 more than 10 = _____

28. 11 more than 2 = _____

29. 17 more than 0 = _____

30. 8 more than 5 = _____

31. $17 - 8 =$ _____

32. $27 - 8 =$ _____

33. $37 - 8 =$ _____

34. $47 - 8 =$ _____

35. $57 - 8 =$ _____

36. $67 - 8 =$ _____

37. $77 - 8 =$ _____

38. $87 - 8 =$ _____

39. $97 - 8 =$ _____

40. $107 - 8 =$ _____

Write as $ and ¢...

41. 153¢ = _____

42. 145¢ = _____

43. 164¢ = _____

44. 110¢ = _____

45. 189¢ = _____

46. 246¢ = _____

47. 351¢ = _____

48. 478¢ = _____

49. 528¢ = _____

50. 846¢ = _____

Jim's Day

Write these key times in Jim's day on the digital watches.

1.   Wakes up at half past seven.

2.   Has breakfast at ten past eight.

3.   Goes walking at five past nine.

4.   Pats a stray dog at ten o'clock.

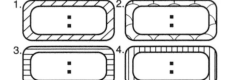

My score: _____ My time: _____ min _____ s

The main thing I didn't understand was _____.

I now know that _____

1. 7 + 3 = _____
2. 4 + 8 = _____
3. 5 + 10 = _____
4. 5 + 6 = _____
5. 9 + 4 = _____
6. 6 + 5 = _____
7. 8 + 4 = _____
8. 5 + 5 = _____
9. 4 + 9 = _____
10. 5 + 7 = _____
11. 5 + 8 = _____
12. 4 + 6 = _____
13. 7 + 4 = _____
14. 4 + 7 = _____
15. 7 + 5 = _____
16. 3 + 8 = _____
17. 6 + 6 = _____
18. 3 + 7 = _____
19. 7 + 7 = _____
20. 8 + 5 = _____
21. _____ + 6 = 13
22. _____ + 5 = 8
23. _____ + 7 = 14
24. _____ + 9 = 13
25. _____ + 3 = 14

26. _____ + 7 = 17
27. _____ + 8 = 16
28. _____ + 2 = 2
29. _____ + 11 = 17
30. _____ + 5 = 12
31. 10 + 7 = _____
32. 11 + 6 = _____
33. 9 + 7 = _____
34. 6 + 11 = _____
35. 5 + 12 = _____
36. 7 + 9 = _____
37. 2 + 3 = _____
38. 10 + 5 = _____
39. 11 + 5 = _____
40. 5 + 11 = _____
41. 7 + 10 = _____
42. 11 + 4 = _____
43. 8 + 9 = _____
44. 12 + 5 = _____
45. 5 + 4 = _____
46. 8 + 8 = _____
47. 13 + 4 = _____
48. 4 + 13 = _____
49. 4 + 5 = _____
50. 9 + 8 = _____

51. 20 + 30 = _____
52. 30 + 40 = _____
53. 50 + 40 = _____
54. 30 + 20 = _____
55. 30 + 50 = _____
56. 40 + 30 = _____
57. 40 + 50 = _____
58. 70 + 30 = _____
59. 60 + 20 = _____
60. 50 + 30 = _____
61. 17 − 5 = _____
62. 17 − 1 = _____
63. 17 − 17 = _____
64. 10 − 3 = _____
65. 17 − 10 = _____
66. 17 − 4 = _____
67. 10 − 8 = _____
68. 17 − 3 = _____
69. 11 − 3 = _____
70. 17 − 9 = _____
71. 17 − 0 = _____
72. 11 − 6 = _____
73. 17 − 8 = _____
74. 17 − 2 = _____
75. 17 − 15 = _____

76. 11 − 4 = _____
77. 17 − 7 = _____
78. 11 − 9 = _____
79. 17 − 11 = _____
80. 17 − 6 = _____
81. 100 − 1 = _____
82. 90 − 1 = _____
83. 80 − 1 = _____
84. 70 − 1 = _____
85. 60 − 1 = _____
86. 50 − 1 = _____
87. 40 − 1 = _____
88. 30 − 1 = _____
89. 20 − 1 = _____
90. 10 − 1 = _____
91. 9 + 8 = _____
92. 19 + 8 = _____
93. 29 + 8 = _____
94. 39 + 8 = _____
95. 49 + 8 = _____
96. 59 + 8 = _____
97. 69 + 8 = _____
98. 79 + 8 = _____
99. 89 + 8 = _____
100. 99 + 8 = _____

My score: _____ My time: _____ min _____ s

The main thing I didn't understand was _____.

I now know that _____
_____.

18 + 0 = 18
17 + 1 = 18
16 + 2 = 18
15 + 3 = 18
14 + 4 = 18
13 + 5 = 18
12 + 6 = 18
11 + 7 = 18
10 + 8 = 18
9 + 9 = 18
8 + 10 = 18
7 + 11 = 18
6 + 12 = 18
5 + 13 = 18
4 + 14 = 18
3 + 15 = 18
2 + 16 = 18
1 + 17 = 18
0 + 18 = 18

18 − 0 = 18
18 − 1 = 17
18 − 2 = 16
18 − 3 = 15
18 − 4 = 14
18 − 5 = 13
18 − 6 = 12
18 − 7 = 11
18 − 8 = 10

9 + 9	7 + 11	2 + 0	8 + 7	3 + 8	12 + 6	6 + 12	7 + 11	1 + 0
0 + 2	11 + 7	3 + 6	7 + 11	8 + 10	9 + 9	0 + 1	9 + 9	8 + 4
6 + 3	7 + 11	6 + 7	9 + 9	5 + 5	4 + 5	8 + 3	10 + 8	8 + 5
7 + 6	9 + 9	8 + 10	10 + 8	3 + 6	0 + 18	9 + 9	8 + 10	5 + 8
8 + 6	4 + 4	4 + 7	5 + 7	6 + 9	1 + 17	7 + 8	4 + 11	7 + 7
2 + 6	6 + 8	4 + 3	5 + 8	7 + 5	17 + 1	7 + 6	7 + 7	6 + 8
5 + 13	13 + 5	15 + 3	3 + 15	16 + 2	2 + 16	8 + 7	8 + 6	10 + 4
4 + 14	4 + 5	7 + 8	6 + 5	9 + 7	12 + 2	3 + 9	7 + 7	8 + 5
14 + 4	5 + 4	6 + 5	8 + 7	3 + 3	7 + 9	8 + 6	4 + 7	4 + 10
13 + 5	5 + 13	6 + 12	12 + 6	11 + 7	7 + 11	8 + 10	10 + 8	9 + 9

18 − 9 = 9
18 − 10 = 8
18 − 11 = 7
18 − 12 = 6
18 − 13 = 5
18 − 14 = 4
18 − 15 = 3
18 − 16 = 2
18 − 17 = 1
18 − 18 = 0

By coloring a path of addition facts that equal eighteen you will lead Bruce and Alison to a lovely picnic spot by Babbling Brook. You can only travel up, down and across, not diagonally.

Jim is hungry. Help him find his way through the maze to the bowl of oatmeal.

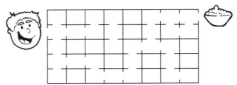

My score: _____ My time: _____ min _____ s

The main thing I didn't understand was _____.

I now know that _____

_____

1. 2 + 6 = _____

2. 12 + 6 = _____

3. 10 + 8 = _____

4. 9 + 8 = _____

5. 7 + 8 = _____

6. 9 + 9 = _____

7. 6 + 12 = _____

8. 8 + 7 = _____

9. 6 + 8 = _____

10. 8 + 10 = _____

11. 8 + 6 = _____

12. 5 + 3 = _____

13. 5 + 13 = _____

14. 7 + 7 = _____

15. 8 + 4 = _____

16. 7 + 7 = _____

17. 8 + 5 = _____

18. 14 + 4 = _____

19. 5 + 7 = _____

20. 10 + 7 = _____

21. 9 + 7 = _____

22. 10 + 8 = _____

23. 9 + 6 = _____

24. 4 + 10 = _____

25. 7 + 11 = _____

26. 7 + 5 = _____

27. 3 + 15 = _____

28. 3 + 5 = _____

29. 7 + 6 = _____

30. 4 + 7 = _____

31. 9 + 5 = _____

32. 10 + 6 = _____

33. 9 + 6 = _____

34. 12 + 6 = _____

35. 2 + 6 = _____

36. 5 + 8 = _____

37. 11 + 7 = _____

38. 5 + 9 = _____

39. 6 + 7 = _____

40. 6 + 5 = _____

Write as $ and ¢...

41. 153¢ = _____

42. 177¢ = _____

43. 192¢ = _____

44. 185¢ = _____

45. 142¢ = _____

46. 163¢ = _____

47. 155¢ = _____

48. 101¢ = _____

49. 120¢ = _____

50. 296¢ = _____

Bruce, Duck and Grub live with Bruce's Mom and Dad in a house on Banana Road. Can you color a path through the grid to it? You must only follow the facts that equal 16.

6 + 5	6 + 6	4 + 11	7 + 7	9 + 5	2 + 14	1 + 15
6 + 2	8 + 7	5 + 1	5 + 9	12 + 4	13 + 3	4 + 5
4 + 12	5 + 11	10 + 6	11 + 5	8 + 8	0 + 1	7 + 2
7 + 3	8 + 5	14 + 1	4 + 6	3 + 12	5 + 4	8 + 6

My score: _____ My time: _____ min _____ s

The main thing I didn't understand was _____.

I now know that _____

_____

1. $3 + 3 =$ _____

2. $3 + 13 =$ _____

3. $10 + 8 =$ _____

4. $8 + 7 =$ _____

5. $9 + 9 =$ _____

6. $7 + 8 =$ _____

7. $7 + 11 =$ _____

8. $8 + 5 =$ _____

9. $6 + 6 =$ _____

10. $7 + 6 =$ _____

11. $9 + 7 =$ _____

12. $5 + 7 =$ _____

13. $9 + 6 =$ _____

14. $7 + 7 =$ _____

15. $8 + 10 =$ _____

16. $11 + 7 =$ _____

17. $9 + 8 =$ _____

18. $8 + 8 =$ _____

19. $8 + 9 =$ _____

20. $6 + 8 =$ _____

21. $4 + 4 =$ _____

22. $8 + 6 =$ _____

23. $7 + 9 =$ _____

24. $7 + 5 =$ _____

25. $9 + 5 =$ _____

26. $5 + 5 =$ _____

27. $6 + 7 =$ _____

28. $5 + 6 =$ _____

29. $4 + 8 =$ _____

30. $2 + 16 =$ _____

31. $8 - 5 =$ _____

32. $18 - 5 =$ _____

33. $28 - 5 =$ _____

34. $38 - 5 =$ _____

35. $48 - 5 =$ _____

36. $58 - 5 =$ _____

37. $68 - 5 =$ _____

38. $78 - 5 =$ _____

39. $88 - 5 =$ _____

40. $98 - 5 =$ _____

41. $18 - 7 =$ _____

42. $18 - 11 =$ _____

43. $18 - 4 =$ _____

44. $18 - 17 =$ _____

45. $18 - 12 =$ _____

46. $18 - 9 =$ _____

47. $18 - 4 =$ _____

48. $18 - 13 =$ _____

49. $18 - 10 =$ _____

50. $18 - 6 =$ _____

Tip

In mathematics, answers that are the names of measuring units should be written with the unit name or abbreviation following. In other cases just the numeral is sufficient.

For example: 2 days + 3 days = 5 days

but

Jim had 6 candies. He ate 4, how many left? Just the answer 2 is sufficient.

My score: _____ My time: _____ min _____ s

The main thing I didn't understand was _____.

I now know that _____

_____.

1. 15 + 3 = _____

2. 8 + 6 = _____

3. 4 + 7 = _____

4. 17 + 1 = _____

5. 8 + 10 = _____

6. 4 + 4 = _____

7. 14 + 4 = _____

8. 5 + 6 = _____

9. 6 + 5 = _____

10. 11 + 7 = _____

11. 5 + 13 = _____

12. 3 + 5 = _____

13. 2 + 16 = _____

14. 5 + 7 = _____

15. 4 + 5 = _____

16. 7 + 11 = _____

17. 3 + 15 = _____

18. 4 + 14 = _____

19. 13 + 5 = _____

20. 5 + 5 = _____

21. 6 + 12 = _____

22. 6 + 4 = _____

23. 7 + 5 = _____

24. 9 + 9 = _____

25. 6 + 7 = _____

26. 8 + 7 = _____

27. 12 + 6 = _____

28. 10 + 8 = _____

29. 7 + 6 = _____

30. 4 + 3 = _____

31. 18 minus 3 = _____

32. 18 minus 13 = _____

33. 18 minus 6 = _____

34. 18 minus 16 = _____

35. 18 minus 5 = _____

36. 18 minus 15 = _____

37. 18 minus 2 = _____

38. 18 minus 12 = _____

39. 18 minus 9 = _____

40. 18 minus 10 = _____

Write as m and cm...

41. 125 cm = ___ m ___ cm

42. 186 cm = ___ m ___ cm

43. 121 cm = ___ m ___ cm

44. 153 cm = ___ m ___ cm

45. 197 cm = ___ m ___ cm

46. 103 cm = ___ m ___ cm

47. 172 cm = ___ m ___ cm

48. 204 cm = ___ m ___ cm

49. 289 cm = ___ m ___ cm

50. 578 cm = ___ m ___ cm

Magic

Think of a number between one and ten. Add four to the number. Now add two more. Take away one. Take away the number you began with. Your answer is 5!

Do you know why Bruce's magic trick works? Change some of the numbers and make up your own magic trick with a different final number.

My score: _____   My time: _____ min _____ s

The main thing I didn't understand was _____.

I now know that _____

_____

1.   6 + 7 = _____

2.   10 + 8 = _____

3.   7 + 6 = _____

4.   8 + 5 = _____

5.   8 + 7 = _____

6.   3 + 15 = _____

7.   7 + 7 = _____

8.   13 + 5 = _____

9.   6 + 8 = _____

10.   10 + 3 = _____

11.   5 + 8 = _____

12.   9 + 9 = _____

13.   7 + 8 = _____

14.   11 + 7 = _____

15.   4 + 9 = _____

16.   9 + 6 = _____

17.   6 + 9 = _____

18.   6 + 12 = _____

19.   8 + 10 = _____

20.   8 + 8 = _____

21.   8 + 9 = _____

22.   12 + 6 = _____

23.   8 + 6 = _____

24.   9 + 7 = _____

25.   7 + 11 = _____

26.   15 – 8 = _____

27.   18 – 9 = _____

28.   15 – 7 = _____

29.   16 – 7 = _____

30.   18 – 6 = _____

31.   15 – 6 = _____

32.   18 – 18 = _____

33.   16 – 8 = _____

34.   16 – 9 = _____

35.   17 – 14 = _____

36.   18 – 10 = _____

37.   15 – 9 = _____

38.   14 – 8 = _____

39.   17 – 12 = _____

40.   18 – 11 = _____

Write as cm...

41.   1 m 23 cm = _____ cm

42.   1 m 38 cm = _____ cm

43.   1 m 70 cm = _____ cm

44.   1 m 8 cm = _____ cm

45.   1 m 91 cm = _____ cm

46.   2 m 1 cm = _____ cm

47.   2 m 17 cm = _____ cm

48.   3 m 45 cm = _____ cm

49.   4 m 53 cm = _____ cm

50.   6 m 81 cm = _____ cm

Circle the coins and bills that aren't denominations in our money.

Color the bills.

  4¢   10¢

13¢   25¢

 🐶 $3   🐶 $5

 $11½ $20

My score: _____   My time: _____ min _____ s

The main thing I didn't understand was _____.

I now know that _____

_____.

 I'm happy   I'm not happy

 OOPS!   I didn't understand

1. 4 + 7 = _____
2. 14 + 4 = _____
3. 9 + 6 = _____
4. 17 + 1 = _____
5. 5 + 4 = _____
6. 5 + 8 = _____
7. 6 + 8 = _____
8. 8 + 6 = _____
9. 5 + 6 = _____
10. 5 + 13 = _____
11. 6 + 6 = _____
12. 6 + 12 = _____
13. 8 + 5 = _____
14. 12 + 6 = _____
15. 9 + 7 = _____
16. 3 + 4 = _____
17. 5 + 7 = _____
18. 8 + 10 = _____
19. 3 + 7 = _____
20. 10 + 8 = _____
21. 7 + 5 = _____
22. 16 + 2 = _____
23. 11 + 7 = _____
24. 7 + 3 = _____
25. 7 + 11 = _____

26. 7 + 9 = _____
27. 4 + 8 = _____
28. 1 + 17 = _____
29. 4 + 14 = _____
30. 6 + 4 = _____
31. 6 + 5 = _____
32. 8 + 7 = _____
33. 7 + 8 = _____
34. 4 + 4 = _____
35. 13 + 5 = _____
36. 7 + 4 = _____
37. 6 + 10 = _____
38. 4 + 6 = _____
39. 7 + 7 = _____
40. 3 + 15 = _____
41. 8 + 8 = _____
42. 2 + 16 = _____
43. 5 + 5 = _____
44. 9 + 9 = _____
45. 5 + 9 = _____
46. 9 + 5 = _____
47. 7 + 6 = _____
48. 6 + 7 = _____
49. 15 + 3 = _____
50. 4 + 3 = _____

51. 30 + 40 = _____
52. 80 + 20 = _____
53. 50 + 40 = _____
54. 60 + 20 = _____
55. 50 + 10 = _____
56. 60 + 40 = _____
57. 40 + 40 = _____
58. 40 + 30 = _____
59. 20 + 60 = _____
60. 40 + 60 = _____
61. 18 – 16 = _____
62. 18 – 6 = _____
63. 13 – 6 = _____
64. 15 – 8 = _____
65. 15 – 7 = _____
66. 15 – 5 = _____
67. 18 – 18 = _____
68. 16 – 8 = _____
69. 18 – 9 = _____
70. 18 – 7 = _____
71. 18 – 17 = _____
72. 18 – 1 = _____
73. 18 – 11 = _____
74. 18 – 13 = _____
75. 18 – 3 = _____

76. 18 – 12 = _____
77. 18 – 2 = _____
78. 18 – 14 = _____
79. 18 – 5 = _____
80. 18 – 15 = _____
81. 23 + 10 = _____
82. 56 + 10 = _____
83. 89 + 10 = _____
84. 34 + 10 = _____
85. 78 + 10 = _____
86. 12 + 10 = _____
87. 45 + 10 = _____
88. 91 + 10 = _____
89. 67 + 10 = _____
90. 1.35 m = ___ cm
91. 1.13 m = ___ cm
92. 1.72 m = ___ cm
93. 1.22 m = ___ cm
94. 1.64 m = ___ cm
95. 1.84 m = ___ cm
96. 1.97 m = ___ cm
97. 1.79 m = ___ cm
98. 1.53 m = ___ cm
99. 1.03 m = ___ cm
100. 1.46 m = ___ cm

My score: _____   My time: _____ min _____ s

The main thing I didn't understand was _____ .

I now know that _____
_____ .

19 + 0 = 19
18 + 1 = 19
17 + 2 = 19
16 + 3 = 19
15 + 4 = 19
14 + 5 = 19
13 + 6 = 19
12 + 7 = 19
11 + 8 = 19
10 + 9 = 19
9 + 10 = 19
8 + 11 = 19
7 + 12 = 19
6 + 13 = 19
5 + 14 = 19
4 + 15 = 19
3 + 16 = 19
2 + 17 = 19
1 + 18 = 19
0 + 19 = 19

19 − 0 = 19
19 − 1 = 18
19 − 2 = 17
19 − 3 = 16
19 − 4 = 15
19 − 5 = 14
19 − 6 = 13
19 − 7 = 12
19 − 8 = 11
19 − 9 = 10
19 − 10 = 9
19 − 11 = 8
19 − 12 = 7

19 − 13 = 6
19 − 14 = 5
19 − 15 = 4
19 − 16 = 3
19 − 17 = 2
19 − 18 = 1
19 − 19 = 0

9 + 10	11 + 8	9 + 10	10 + 9	6 + 13	7 + 12	9 + 7	4 + 5	2 + 9
9 + 2	6 + 8	10 + 7	4 + 4	11 + 7	9 + 10	5 + 5	5 + 3	8 + 7
12 + 7	13 + 6	6 + 13	15 + 4	14 + 5	10 + 9	5 + 6	5 + 10	4 + 6
7 + 12	5 + 4	5 + 11	6 + 2	5 + 12	6 + 1	6 + 4	6 + 3	5 + 13
8 + 11	4 + 3	19 + 0	0 + 19	1 + 18	18 + 1	17 + 2	2 + 17	3 + 16
11 + 8	4 + 2	1 + 18	4 + 7	10 + 3	9 + 4	4 + 9	3 + 7	16 + 3
10 + 9	9 + 10	18 + 1	4 + 11	6 + 13	5 + 14	14 + 5	15 + 4	4 + 15
8 + 6	4 + 8	4 + 12	5 + 1	13 + 6	5 + 8	8 + 6	7 + 3	4 + 6
4 + 1	4 + 13	4 + 14	5 + 7	12 + 7	7 + 12	11 + 8	8 + 11	10 + 9
4 + 9	5 + 2	5 + 8	5 + 9	4 + 10	8 + 5	7 + 7	6 + 4	9 + 10

Jim is tiptoeing softly away from Tulip Island.
He went there to do some exploring and
found himself captured by Boffo, the giant
who lives there.

Now, while Boffo sleeps, Jim is sneaking away to
his boat on the other side of the island.

Show him the way through the forest by coloring a
path of facts that equal nineteen. You can only
travel up, down and across, not diagonally.

My score: _____ My time: _____ min _____ s

The main thing I didn't understand was _____.

I now know that _____

_____.

1. 8 + 7 = _____

2. 12 + 7 = _____

3. 7 + 11 = _____

4. 10 + 9 = _____

5. 2 + 17 = _____

6. 7 + 5 = _____

7. 15 + 4 = _____

8. 11 + 7 = _____

9. 4 + 15 = _____

10. 10 + 8 = _____

11. 8 + 9 = _____

12. 7 + 12 = _____

13. 9 + 10 = _____

14. 5 + 14 = _____

15. 8 + 10 = _____

16. 6 + 6 = _____

17. 14 + 5 = _____

18. 9 + 7 = _____

19. 9 + 8 = _____

20. 9 + 9 = _____

21. 11 + 8 = _____

22. 21 + 8 = _____

23. 31 + 8 = _____

24. 41 + 8 = _____

25. 51 + 8 = _____

26. 61 + 8 = _____

27. 71 + 8 = _____

28. 81 + 8 = _____

29. 91 + 8 = _____

30. 101 + 8 = _____

31. 19 minus 6 = _____

32. 19 minus 16 = _____

33. 19 minus 10 = _____

34. 19 minus 9 = _____

35. 19 minus 3 = _____

36. 19 minus 13 = _____

37. 19 minus 4 = _____

38. 19 minus 14 = _____

39. 19 minus 1 = _____

40. 19 minus 11 = _____

41. 7 + 9 = _____

42. 17 + 9 = _____

43. 27 + 9 = _____

44. 37 + 9 = _____

45. 47 + 9 = _____

46. 57 + 9 = _____

47. 67 + 9 = _____

48. 77 + 9 = _____

49. 87 + 9 = _____

50. 97 + 9 = _____

Perimeter means the distance around the outside of a shape.

Find the perimeter of these shapes by using a ruler. Write your answers on the lines in centimeters.

Robert Rectangle = _____ cm

Tom Triangle =

_____ cm

My score: _____ My time: _____ min _____ s

The main thing I didn't understand was _____.

I now know that _____

_____.

1. $13 + 6 =$ _____
2. $7 + 6 =$ _____
3. $8 + 7 =$ _____
4. $7 + 8 =$ _____
5. $5 + 14 =$ _____
6. $8 + 9 =$ _____
7. $9 + 10 =$ _____
8. $9 + 6 =$ _____
9. $6 + 7 =$ _____
10. $8 + 11 =$ _____
11. $8 + 5 =$ _____
12. $9 + 9 =$ _____
13. $7 + 12 =$ _____
14. $5 + 8 =$ _____
15. $4 + 15 =$ _____
16. $6 + 13 =$ _____
17. $9 + 8 =$ _____

18. $8 + 4 =$ _____
19. $14 + 5 =$ _____
20. $6 + 3 =$ _____
21. $16 + 3 =$ _____
22. $8 + 8 =$ _____
23. $10 + 9 =$ _____
24. $15 + 4 =$ _____
25. $10 + 7 =$ _____
26. $6 + 8 =$ _____
27. $11 + 8 =$ _____
28. $8 + 6 =$ _____
29. $12 + 7 =$ _____
30. $6 + 7 =$ _____

Write the total amount...

31. $1 + 20¢ + 5¢ = _____
32. $1 + 50¢ + 10¢ = _____
33. $1 + 50¢ + 20¢ = _____

34. $1 + 20¢ + 10¢ = _____
35. $1 + 50¢ + 5¢ = _____
36. $2 + 50¢ + 20¢ = _____
37. $2 + $1 + 5¢ = _____
38. $2 + 5¢ = _____
39. $2 + $1 + 20¢ = _____
40. $2 + $1 + 50¢ = _____
41. $100 - 20 =$ _____
42. $100 - 70 =$ _____
43. $100 - 30 =$ _____
44. $100 - 80 =$ _____
45. $100 - 40 =$ _____
46. $100 - 60 =$ _____
47. $100 - 10 =$ _____
48. $100 - 90 =$ _____
49. $100 - 50 =$ _____
50. $100 - 100 =$ _____

Measuring the perimeter of irregular shapes with curved lines can be done quite easily using string. It is a good idea to tape your string to a beginning point.

Measure the perimeter of the blob in centimeters.

Bob the Blob = _____ cm

My score: _____ My time: _____ min _____ s

The main thing I didn't understand was _____.

I now know that _____
_____

I'm happy

I'm not happy

OOPS!

I didn't understand

     Math Speed Tests – Book 1   © World Teachers Press® – www.worldteacherspress.com

1.   13 + 6 = _____

2.   4 + 8 = _____

3.   2 + 9 = _____

4.   9 + 10 = _____

5.   6 + 7 = _____

6.   15 + 4 = _____

7.   9 + 3 = _____

8.   8 + 6 = _____

9.   10 + 9 = _____

10.   5 + 6 = _____

11.   6 + 8 = _____

12.   3 + 16 = _____

13.   6 + 5 = _____

14.   7 + 7 = _____

15.   11 + 8 = _____

16.   4 + 7 = _____

17.   8 + 7 = _____

18.   12 + 7 = _____

19.   7 + 4 = _____

20.   7 + 8 = _____

21.   3 + 8 = _____

22.   7 + 12 = _____

23.   16 + 3 = _____

24.   7 + 11 = _____

25.   6 + 13 = _____

26.   2 + 17 = _____

27.   9 + 2 = _____

28.   8 + 4 = _____

29.   7 + 6 = _____

30.   8 + 11 = _____

31.   5 + 7 = _____

32.   6 + 9 = _____

33.   4 + 15 = _____

34.   7 + 5 = _____

35.   9 + 6 = _____

36.   16 + 3 = _____

37.   8 + 3 = _____

38.   18 + 1 = _____

39.   6 + 6 = _____

40.   17 + 2 = _____

41.   600 + 40 + 3 = _____

42.   300 + 70 + 4 = _____

43.   800 + 90 + 8 = _____

44.   500 + 80 + 5 = _____

45.   400 + 50 + 9 = _____

46.   900 + 60 + 1 = _____

47.   200 + 10 + 6 = _____

48.   500 + 60 + 1 = _____

49.   100 + 20 + 7 = _____

50.   700 + 30 + 2 = _____

Here are some more perimeters for you to measure.

Ben Blob = _____ cm

Bill Blob = _____ cm

My score: _____   My time: _____ min _____ s

The main thing I didn't understand was _____.

I now know that _____

_____.

1. 1 + 18 = _____

2. 7 + 6 = _____

3. 14 + 5 = _____

4. 6 + 7 = _____

5. 2 + 17 = _____

6. 7 + 7 = _____

7. 13 + 6 = _____

8. 3 + 8 = _____

9. 0 + 19 = _____

10. 17 + 2 = _____

11. 8 + 7 = _____

12. 7 + 8 = _____

13. 3 + 16 = _____

14. 5 + 14 = _____

15. 6 + 5 = _____

16. 19 + 0 = _____

17. 5 + 6 = _____

18. 12 + 7 = _____

19. 7 + 6 = _____

20. 6 + 7 = _____

21. 18 + 1 = _____

22. 7 + 12 = _____

23. 5 + 7 = _____

24. 16 + 3 = _____

25. 7 + 5 = _____

26. 5 + 8 = _____

27. 4 + 15 = _____

28. 8 + 5 = _____

29. 6 + 13 = _____

30. 15 + 4 = _____

31. 10 – 3 = _____

32. 18 – 4 = _____

33. 14 – 3 = _____

34. 10 – 4 = _____

35. 17 – 4 = _____

36. 15 – 3 = _____

37. 11 – 4 = _____

38. 16 – 4 = _____

39. 11 – 3 = _____

40. 16 – 3 = _____

41. 12 – 4 = _____

42. 9 – 3 = _____

43. 12 – 3 = _____

44. 17 – 3 = _____

45. 13 – 4 = _____

46. 18 – 3 = _____

47. 14 – 4 = _____

48. 13 – 3 = _____

49. 15 – 4 = _____

50. 19 – 3 = _____

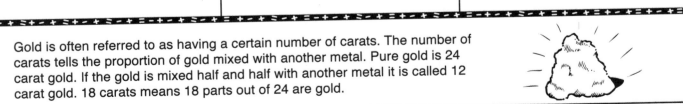

Gold is often referred to as having a certain number of carats. The number of carats tells the proportion of gold mixed with another metal. Pure gold is 24 carat gold. If the gold is mixed half and half with another metal it is called 12 carat gold. 18 carats means 18 parts out of 24 are gold.

My score: _____ My time: _____ min _____ s

The main thing I didn't understand was _____.

I now know that _____

_____.

Math Speed Tests – Book 1

1. 9 + 3 = _____	26. 13 + 6 = _____	51. 9 + 9 = _____	76. 14 – 9 = _____
2. 8 + 5 = _____	27. 4 + 3 = _____	52. 9 + 2 = _____	77. 14 – 7 = _____
3. 9 + 6 = _____	28. 4 + 5 = _____	53. 11 + 6 = _____	78. 19 – 10 = _____
4. 16 + 3 = _____	29. 8 + 7 = _____	54. 7 + 2 = _____	79. 15 – 7 = _____
5. 8 + 10 = _____	30. 7 + 8 = _____	55. 4 + 9 = _____	80. 14 – 11 = _____
6. 6 + 9 = _____	31. 4 + 8 = _____	56. 3 + 16 = _____	81. 15 – 8 = _____
7. 6 + 7 = _____	32. 4 + 15 = _____	57. 9 + 4 = _____	82. 19 – 12 = _____
8. 7 + 6 = _____	33. 5 + 4 = _____	58. 5 + 2 = _____	83. 15 – 11 = _____
9. 3 + 9 = _____	34. 7 + 4 = _____	59. 8 + 4 = _____	84. 15 – 12 = _____
10. 18 + 1 = _____	35. 15 + 4 = _____	60. 10 + 8 = _____	85. 19 – 5 = _____
11. 9 + 7 = _____	36. 4 + 7 = _____	61. 19 – 6 = _____	86. 17 – 11 = _____
12. 7 + 5 = _____	37. 7 + 11 = _____	62. 13 – 6 = _____	87. 16 – 11 = _____
13. 5 + 14 = _____	38. 9 + 5 = _____	63. 13 – 7 = _____	88. 19 – 11 = _____
14. 3 + 7 = _____	39. 14 + 5 = _____	64. 19 – 13 = _____	89. 15 – 9 = _____
15. 5 + 7 = _____	40. 2 + 5 = _____	65. 15 – 8 = _____	90. 18 – 11 = _____
16. 9 + 8 = _____	41. 6 + 5 = _____	66. 14 – 6 = _____	91. 100 + 32 = _____
17. 8 + 9 = _____	42. 5 + 6 = _____	67. 19 – 7 = _____	92. 200 + 45 = _____
18. 7 + 3 = _____	43. 1 + 18 = _____	68. 12 – 11 = _____	93. 700 + 28 = _____
19. 7 + 10 = _____	44. 7 + 7 = _____	69. 19 – 14 = _____	94. 900 + 67 = _____
20. 6 + 4 = _____	45. 11 + 7 = _____	70. 13 – 11 = _____	95. 500 + 63 = _____
21. 17 + 2 = _____	46. 8 + 8 = _____	71. 19 – 8 = _____	96. 800 + 45 = _____
22. 5 + 10 = _____	47. 2 + 9 = _____	72. 14 – 8 = _____	97. 400 + 52 = _____
23. 4 + 6 = _____	48. 6 + 8 = _____	73. 19 – 15 = _____	98. 600 + 99 = _____
24. 3 + 8 = _____	49. 8 + 6 = _____	74. 19 – 4 = _____	99. 800 + 56 = _____
25. 8 + 3 = _____	50. 2 + 17 = _____	75. 19 – 9 = _____	100. 300 + 89 = _____

My score: _____   My time: _____ min _____ s

The main thing I didn't understand was _____.

I now know that _____
_____.

18 + 2	6 + 6	5 + 12	6 + 8	10 + 5	7 + 7	9 + 2	9 + 1	9 + 3
13 + 7	4 + 4	12 + 5	9 + 6	3 + 10	7 + 6	10 + 4	0 + 9	9 + 4
15 + 5	5 + 7	11 + 9	12 + 8	13 + 7	14 + 6	15 + 5	14 + 6	8 + 8
6 + 14	13 + 7	8 + 12	8 + 5	4 + 4	8 + 7	6 + 6	6 + 14	9 + 5
6 + 2	2 + 7	3 + 8	9 + 6	6 + 9	12 + 8	13 + 7	7 + 13	9 + 6
7 + 13	8 + 12	12 + 8	11 + 9	10 + 9	8 + 12	5 + 5	10 + 6	9 + 7
13 + 7	10 + 5	13 + 2	9 + 11	19 + 1	0 + 20	10 + 7	6 + 7	9 + 8
14 + 6	6 + 14	12 + 3	8 + 6	3 + 3	10 + 8	7 + 6	7 + 9	9 + 9
8 + 7	5 + 15	15 + 5	16 + 4	7 + 7	2 + 18	18 + 2	19 + 1	1 + 1
9 + 6	10 + 5	11 + 4	4 + 16	17 + 3	3 + 17	2 + 2	1 + 19	0 + 20

20 + 0 = 20
19 + 1 = 20
18 + 2 = 20
17 + 3 = 20
16 + 4 = 20
15 + 5 = 20
14 + 6 = 20
13 + 7 = 20
12 + 8 = 20
11 + 9 = 20
10 + 10 = 20
9 + 11 = 20
8 + 12 = 20
7 + 13 = 20
6 + 14 = 20
5 + 15 = 20
4 + 16 = 20
3 + 17 = 20
2 + 18 = 20
1 + 19 = 20
0 + 20 = 20

20 − 0 = 20
20 − 1 = 19
20 − 2 = 18
20 − 3 = 17
20 − 4 = 16
20 − 5 = 15
20 − 6 = 14
20 − 7 = 13
20 − 8 = 12
20 − 9 = 11
20 − 10 = 10
20 − 11 = 9

20 − 12 = 8
20 − 13 = 7
20 − 14 = 6
20 − 15 = 5
20 − 16 = 4
20 − 17 = 3
20 − 18 = 2
20 − 19 = 1
20 − 20 = 0

Help Maggie Magpie find her way to her nest. She must fly through the Twenty Kilometer Forest.

Color the facts that equal twenty and you will show her the way. You can only travel up, down and across, not diagonally.

My score: _____ My time: _____ min _____ s

The main thing I didn't understand was _____.

I now know that _____

_____

1. 9 + 3 = _____
2. 8 + 12 = _____
3. 6 + 6 = _____
4. 7 + 13 = _____
5. 9 + 4 = _____
6. 13 + 7 = _____
7. 7 + 7 = _____
8. 10 + 5 = _____
9. 9 + 11 = _____
10. 8 + 8 = _____
11. 9 + 5 = _____
12. 10 + 10 = _____
13. 10 + 6 = _____
14. 9 + 9 = _____
15. 13 + 7 = _____
16. 9 + 6 = _____
17. 6 + 14 = _____

18. 10 + 7 = _____
19. 3 + 3 = _____
20. 14 + 6 = _____
21. 9 + 8 = _____
22. 10 + 8 = _____
23. 9 + 7 = _____
24. 16 + 4 = _____
25. 10 + 9 = _____
26. 10 – 7 = _____
27. 20 – 7 = _____
28. 10 – 4 = _____
29. 20 – 4 = _____
30. 10 – 9 = _____
31. 20 – 9 = _____
32. 10 – 1 = _____
33. 20 – 1 = _____
34. 10 – 5 = _____

35. 20 – 5 = _____
36. 10 – 3 = _____
37. 20 – 3 = _____
38. 10 – 2 = _____
39. 20 – 2 = _____

	Total =	Boys	Girls
40.	17 =	____	10
41.	14 =	____	8
42.	10 =	____	3
43.	18 =	11	____
44.	13 =	____	7
45.	11 =	5	____
46.	19 =	____	9
47.	15 =	____	7
48.	12 =	8	____
49.	16 =	8	____
50.	20 =	9	____

Nautical Measures

The depth of water at sea is often calculated in fathoms.

- 1 fathom = approximately 1 m 80 cm (1.8 m) or 6 feet
- 100 fathoms = 1 cable length
- 10 cable lengths = 1 international nautical mile
- 60 nautical miles = 1 degree of a great circle of the earth

My score: _____ My time: _____ min _____ s

The main thing I didn't understand was _____.

I now know that _____
_____.

1. 15 + 5 = _____

2. 12 + 1 = _____

3. 8 + 7 = _____

4. 7 + 7 = _____

5. 8 + 5 = _____

6. 6 + 14 = _____

7. 7 + 8 = _____

8. 8 + 2 = _____

9. 8 + 12 = _____

10. 9 + 5 = _____

11. 9 + 7 = _____

12. 9 + 8 = _____

13. 5 + 15 = _____

14. 7 + 6 = _____

15. 3 + 17 = _____

16. 9 + 4 = _____

17. 6 + 8 = _____

18. 17 + 3 = _____

19. 8 + 6 = _____

20. 9 + 3 = _____

21. 4 + 6 = _____

22. 14 + 6 = _____

23. 7 + 8 = _____

24. 9 + 9 = _____

25. 8 + 8 = _____

26. 20 – 5 = _____

27. 20 – 13 = _____

28. 20 – 3 = _____

29. 20 – 2 = _____

30. 20 – 6 = _____

31. 20 – 4 = _____

32. 20 – 1 = _____

33. 20 – 9 = _____

34. 20 – 8 = _____

35. 20 – 10 = _____

36. 20 – 7 = _____

37. 20 – 11 = _____

38. 20 – 14 = _____

39. 20 – 16 = _____

40. 20 – 12 = _____

41. 30 + 20 + 6 = _____

42. 30 + 30 + 7 = _____

43. 10 + 20 + 3 = _____

44. 40 + 20 + 3 = _____

45. 10 + 30 + 9 = _____

46. 30 + 40 + 9 = _____

47. 50 + 20 + 8 = _____

48. 20 + 50 + 6 = _____

49. 20 + 20 + 7 = _____

50. 20 + 30 + 1 = _____

"An apple a day keeps the doctor away," is an old saying.

How many apples would you have to eat in a year to avoid the doctor?

Eat apples.

_____ apples

My score: _____ My time: _____ min _____ s

The main thing I didn't understand was _____.

I now know that _____.

1.   3 + 17 = _____

2.   7 + 9 = _____

3.   0 + 20 = _____

4.   7 + 7 = _____

5.   13 + 7 = _____

6.   17 + 3 = _____

7.   6 + 7 = _____

8.   9 + 8 = _____

9.   8 + 12 = _____

10.   4 + 15 = _____

11.   7 + 6 = _____

12.   5 + 8 = _____

13.   3 + 11 = _____

14.   16 + 4 = _____

15.   8 + 6 = _____

16.   9 + 1 = _____

17.   9 + 11 = _____

18.   4 + 6 = _____

19.   5 + 15 = _____

20.   8 + 7 = _____

21.   7 + 8 = _____

22.   8 + 2 = _____

23.   8 + 12 = _____

24.   7 + 9 = _____

25.   11 + 9 = _____

26.   7 + 4 = _____

27.   15 + 5 = _____

28.   5 + 6 = _____

29.   8 + 11 = _____

30.   4 + 16 = _____

31.   3 + 2 + 4 = _____

32.   4 + 2 + 6 = _____

33.   6 + 5 + 4 = _____

34.   2 + 1 + 4 = _____

35.   5 + 5 + 4 = _____

36.   6 + 7 + 3 = _____

37.   5 + 9 + 2 = _____

38.   8 + 4 + 2 = _____

39.   7 + 1 + 2 = _____

40.   6 + 3 + 4 = _____

41.   23 + 10 = _____

42.   23 + 20 = _____

43.   54 + 30 = _____

44.   42 + 20 = _____

45.   56 + 40 = _____

46.   40 + 46 = _____

47.   30 + 32 = _____

48.   50 + 27 = _____

49.   10 + 36 = _____

50.   40 + 48 = _____

Do you know the numbers?

_____ is company   _____ little pigs

_____ is a crowd   _____ bears

_____ blind mice   _____ billy goats gruff

A bird in the hand is worth _____ in the bush.

My score: _____   My time: _____ min _____ s

The main thing I didn't understand was _____.

I now know that _____
_____

1. 8 + 9 = _____

2. 9 + 9 = _____

3. 7 + 13 = _____

4. 9 + 10 = _____

5. 8 + 7 = _____

6. 9 + 11 = _____

7. 14 + 6 = _____

8. 7 + 8 = _____

9. 6 + 14 = _____

10. 8 + 8 = _____

11. 11 + 9 = _____

12. 8 + 7 = _____

13. 5 + 15 = _____

14. 9 + 6 = _____

15. 2 + 18 = _____

16. 6 + 9 = _____

17. 16 + 4 = _____

18. 7 + 6 = _____

19. 10 + 10 = _____

20. 8 + 10 = _____

21. 8 + 6 = _____

22. 12 + 8 = _____

23. 8 + 5 = _____

24. 11 + 8 = _____

25. 18 + 2 = _____

26. 6 + 8 = _____

27. 4 + 16 = _____

28. 9 + 7 = _____

29. 9 + 5 = _____

30. 15 + 5 = _____

31. 10 – 8 = _____

32. 20 – 8 = _____

33. 10 – 4 = _____

34. 20 – 4 = _____

35. 10 – 9 = _____

36. 20 – 9 = _____

37. 10 – 5 = _____

38. 20 – 5 = _____

39. 10 – 3 = _____

40. 20 – 3 = _____

41. 40 + 70 = _____

42. 30 + 20 = _____

43. 80 + 60 = _____

44. 70 + 70 = _____

45. 60 + 80 = _____

46. 30 + 90 = _____

47. 50 + 60 = _____

48. 70 + 60 = _____

49. 60 + 70 = _____

50. 60 + 40 = _____

Learn your mathematical abbreviations.

second(s) =	s	week(s) =	wk(s)	gram(s) =	g
minute(s) =	min	centimeter(s) =	cm	kilogram(s) =	kg
year(s) =	yr(s)	meter(s) =	m	liter(s) =	L
month(s) =	mo(s)	kilometer(s) =	km	milliliter(s) =	mL

My score: _____   My time: _____ min _____ s

The main thing I didn't understand was _____.

I now know that _____

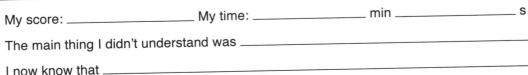

1. 2 + 8 = _____
2. 9 + 11 = _____
3. 7 + 4 = _____
4. 0 + 20 = _____
5. 4 + 8 = _____
6. 4 + 7 = _____
7. 3 + 7 = _____
8. 7 + 3 = _____
9. 17 + 3 = _____
10. 6 + 5 = _____
11. 4 + 16 = _____
12. 5 + 6 = _____
13. 6 + 4 = _____
14. 8 + 12 = _____
15. 8 + 2 = _____
16. 8 + 3 = _____
17. 8 + 4 = _____
18. 19 + 1 = _____
19. 4 + 6 = _____
20. 6 + 14 = _____
21. 20 − 1 = _____
22. 20 − 7 = _____
23. 20 − 3 = _____
24. 20 − 6 = _____
25. 20 − 8 = _____

26. 20 − 2 = _____
27. 20 − 5 = _____
28. 20 − 9 = _____
29. 20 − 10 = _____
30. 20 − 4 = _____
31. 5 + 7 = _____
32. 3 + 17 = _____
33. 5 + 5 = _____
34. 7 + 5 = _____
35. 14 + 6 = _____
36. 2 + 9 = _____
37. 6 + 7 = _____
38. 20 + 0 = _____
39. 9 + 3 = _____
40. 13 + 7 = _____
41. 7 + 6 = _____
42. 3 + 9 = _____
43. 3 + 8 = _____
44. 12 + 8 = _____
45. 18 + 2 = _____
46. 6 + 6 = _____
47. 10 + 10 = _____
48. 9 + 1 = _____
49. 9 + 2 = _____
50. 15 + 5 = _____

51. 20 − 15 = _____
52. 20 − 11 = _____
53. 20 − 14 = _____
54. 20 − 20 = _____
55. 20 − 19 = _____
56. 20 − 16 = _____
57. 20 − 12 = _____
58. 20 − 17 = _____
59. 20 − 18 = _____
60. 20 − 13 = _____
61. 8 + 5 = _____
62. 8 + 6 = _____
63. 6 + 8 = _____
64. 2 + 18 = _____
65. 5 + 8 = _____
66. 11 + 9 = _____
67. 9 + 4 = _____
68. 7 + 7 = _____
69. 8 + 7 = _____
70. 16 + 4 = _____
71. 7 + 8 = _____
72. 7 + 13 = _____
73. 9 + 6 = _____
74. 5 + 9 = _____
75. 8 + 8 = _____

76. 1 + 19 = _____
77. 3 + 10 = _____
78. 5 + 15 = _____
79. 7 + 9 = _____
80. 4 + 9 = _____
81. 11 − 3 = _____
82. 16 − 8 = _____
83. 13 − 6 = _____
84. 15 − 7 = _____
85. 12 − 4 = _____
86. 17 − 9 = _____
87. 14 − 8 = _____
88. 13 − 5 = _____
89. 14 − 6 = _____
90. 18 − 5 = _____
91. 100 − 1 = _____
92. 200 − 1 = _____
93. 300 − 1 = _____
94. 400 − 1 = _____
95. 500 − 1 = _____
96. 600 − 1 = _____
97. 700 − 1 = _____
98. 800 − 1 = _____
99. 900 − 1 = _____
100. 1,000 − 1 = _____

My score: _____   My time: _____ min _____ s

The main thing I didn't understand was _____.

I now know that _____

1. 7 + 7 = _____
2. 9 + 9 = _____
3. 3 + 3 = _____
4. 4 + 4 = _____
5. 6 + 6 = _____
6. 10 + 10 = _____
7. 1 + 1 = _____
8. 0 + 0 = _____
9. 5 + 5 = _____
10. 2 + 2 = _____
11. 8 + 8 = _____
12. 0 + 8 = _____
13. 8 + 1 = _____
14. 9 + 2 = _____
15. 3 + 6 = _____
16. 7 + 9 = _____
17. 8 + 12 = _____
18. 4 + 14 = _____
19. 6 + 12 = _____
20. 10 + 3 = _____
21. 9 + 4 = _____
22. 8 + 6 = _____
23. 10 + 5 = _____
24. 19 + 1 = _____
25. 0 + 20 = _____

26. 15 – 8 = _____
27. 6 – 2 = _____
28. 5 – 3 = _____
29. 9 – 6 = _____
30. 19 – 5 = _____
31. 15 – 9 = _____
32. 16 – 7 = _____
33. 7 – 7 = _____
34. 10 – 3 = _____
35. 18 – 6 = _____
36. 20 – 10 = _____
37. 18 – 9 = _____
38. 16 – 8 = _____
39. 14 – 7 = _____
40. 12 – 6 = _____
41. 10 – 5 = _____
42. 8 – 4 = _____
43. 6 – 3 = _____
44. 4 – 2 = _____
45. 2 – 1 = _____
46. 14 + 6 = _____
47. 18 + 2 = _____
48. 3 + 17 = _____
49. 0 + 0 = _____
50. 10 + 9 = _____

51. 6 + 8 = _____
52. 10 – 3 = _____
53. 4 + 9 = _____
54. 12 + 7 = _____
55. 5 + 13 = _____
56. 18 – 3 = _____
57. 9 + 8 = _____
58. 12 – 4 = _____
59. 16 + 4 = _____
60. 16 – 4 = _____
61. 11 + 5 = _____
62. 11 – 5 = _____
63. 10 + 0 = _____
64. 10 – 0 = _____
65. 3 + 17 = _____
66. 17 – 3 = _____
67. 2 + 16 = _____
68. 16 – 2 = _____
69. 5 + 15 = _____
70. 15 – 5 = _____
71. 12 + 8 = _____
72. 12 – 8 = _____
73. 14 + 6 = _____
74. 14 – 6 = _____
75. 13 + 5 = _____

76. 19 + 5 = _____
77. 13 + 10 = _____
78. 6 + 7 = _____
79. 29 + 13 = _____
80. 4 + 16 = _____
81. 7 + 17 = _____
82. 9 + 19 = _____
83. 8 + 8 = _____
84. 17 – 6 = _____
85. 27 – 16 = _____
86. 37 – 26 = _____
87. 47 – 36 = _____
88. 12 + 7 = _____
89. 14 + 7 = _____
90. 16 + 7 = _____
91. 18 + 6 = _____
92. 30 – 15 = _____
93. 17 – 8 = _____
94. 25 – 9 = _____
95. 100 – 10 = _____
96. 100 – 35 = _____
97. 100 – 40 = _____
98. 100 – 60 = _____
99. 26 + 14 = _____
100. 18 + 18 = _____

My score: _____ My time: _____ min _____ s

The main thing I didn't understand was _____.

I now know that _____

Test	1	2	3	4	5	6	7	8	11	12	13	14	16	17	18	19	21
1.	1	9	9	8	9	10	9	10	10	7	8	10	9	11	11	12	13
2.	5	7	7	9	10	9	10	10	9	10	5	11	12	12	12	10	11
3.	3	8	8	6	8	9	9	9	11	11	1	10	11	10	10	11	13
4.	9	6	9	8	10	6	8	10	10	8	7	9	10	12	12	12	12
5.	5	9	5	7	9	10	10	7	8	10	4	11	12	10	11	9	13
6.	7	7	8	8	10	6	8	8	11	11	0	8	8	11	12	7	11
7.	9	5	7	7	8	9	9	10	6	10	6	11	11	10	10	12	10
8.	7	8	9	5	7	10	10	5	5	9	3	10	11	9	12	12	12
9.	4	9	6	7	9	6	9	8	11	10	2	8	12	11	10	10	13
10.	8	4	8	8	6	10	10	9	7	11	9	11	8	6	12	11	12
11.	9	3	6	7	10	5	8	4	10	11	11	9	12	12	7	12	11
12.	4	7	9	8	7	6	8	8	11	10	10	8	10	4	11	10	10
13.	9	6	6	9	10	7	10	7	8	11	11	11	9	12	12	12	13
14.	6	8	9	5	10	7	9	10	11	10	9	7	7	11	12	11	13
15.	8	7	6	7	6	9	10	9	11	11	10	12	12	11	12	10	
16.	9	9	9	9	8	4	8	7	11	7	7	6	12	10	10	10	13
17.	7	7	8	6	10	10	10	8	10	11	10	11	11	12	12	12	12
18.	8	6	8	7	9	7	8	10	7	9	11	9	12	8	11	11	13
19.	5	5	7	3	8	10	9	9	11	11	9	10	10	12	8	12	12
20.	9	9	6	9	9	9	10	10	10	8	5	11	12	9	12	8	11
21.	2	8	9	6	10	6	7	7	8	10	10	8	6	6	7	12	13
22.	8	9	7	5	7	10	10	10	11	11	11	7	12	11	12	5	13
23.	7	5	7	9	10	5	10	7	9	10	11	11	11	12	9	9	11
24.	8	6	8	4	6	6	9	10	9	11	5	9	9	8	12	9	9
25.	4	5	9	2	10	9	9	9	11	7	11	11	12	7	9	7	13
26.	7	9	8	9	7	10	10	10	10	11	10	10	11	12	12	11	10
27.	6	8	9	6	9	3	8	7	5	11	8	11	12	12	11	12	13
28.	7	6	7	9	10	10	9	9	11	9	11	5	9	9	12	10	12
29.	9	8	8	8	10	9	5	9	11	11	11	9	7	12	9	11	11
30.	6	8	9	7	5	9	10	8	11	9	10	9	12	8	11	5	9
31.	6	7	9	8	8	7	8	2	9	11	10	7	12	8	12	9	13
32.	9	9	7	4	4	10	9	2	11	10	11	8	11	12	8	8	13
33.	9	6	4	7	10	7	5	7	7	8	9	6	12	12	4	12	8
34.	6	7	9	5	5	10	2	1	10	11	7	4	12	9	3	10	12
35.	8	8	8	6	10	7	4	0	9	10	11	5	10	12	10	10	13
36.	4	6	6	2	9	10	0	2	11	11	9	1	12	7	7	8	12
37.	8	7	8	5	10	6	1	1	8	10	9	3	7	10	9	12	13
38.	7	8	8	6	5	7	3	1	11	11	10	2	12	12	5	9	11
39.	9	5	6	5	4	7	6	1	7	11	11	3	11	12	6	11	11
40.	5	9	2	7	5	10	7	3	6	10	11	9	12	7	11	6	13
41.	8	4	3	4	6	3	3	23	20	7	21	32	11	27	12	3	9
42.	3	6	4	2	2	2	1	26	30	3	31	71	3	57	22	3	59
43.	6	7	5	1	7	5	3	24	50	6	41	15	10	17	32	8	99
44.	2	5	6	1	5	4	3	27	40	10	51	47	5	47	42	4	89
45.	5	1	7	2	1	6	2	29	60	4	61	83	6	37	52	4	49
46.	4	3	2	2	4	0	1	34	70	9	71	65	8	77	62	2	29
47.	7	2	3	5	3	4	2	38	80	2	81	58	3	87	72	5	79
48.	0	0	4	1	5	3	2	35	70	5	91	42	7	107	82	5	39
49.	1	1	6	2	3	7	1	31	80	1	101	24	4	97	92	7	69
50.	7	3	7	2	6	1	2	30	60	8	7	69	9	67	102	6	19

Test	22	23	24	26	27	28	29	31	32	33	34	36	37	38	39	41	42	43
1.	12	13	3	11	12	7	11	10	13	15	13	13	13	15	14	17	16	17
2.	13	12	7	14	14	13	14	14	15	14	13	16	16	16	10	17	15	13
3.	11	13	4	12	13	12	14	15	12	11	13	11	16	9	15	16	17	12
4.	13	11	8	14	13	14	7	14	11	15	15	16	14	16	12	14	14	10
5.	10	13	2	12	14	13	13	12	15	14	12	14	11	16	16	17	13	17
6.	13	13	5	10	11	11	14	15	15	13	15	12	6	15	16	15	17	12
7.	13	10	11	14	14	14	9	14	12	15	11	16	16	16	13	10	14	17
8.	12	9	1	11	11	12	12	15	15	15	15	14	16	14	15	17	16	13
9.	10	13	6	10	14	14	12	15	11	12	12	11	16	16	12	14	12	9
10.	13	13	12	14	11	13	14	11	15	15	9	16	10	14	9	17	17	17
11.	11	9	13	14	14	12	14	15	11	12	15	13	12	16	16	16	16	10
12.	11	13	12	11	11	14	9	14	15	15	15	16	16	14	14	12	12	9
13.	12	12	13	14	14	12	12	11	10	14	15	13	13	16	11	16	17	17
14.	12	8	11	14	14	11	11	15	11	15	11	15	16	16	16	12	15	13
15.	13	10	10	13	12	14	14	11	15	14	15	15	12	13	13	17	13	11
16.	10	13	13	11	14	12	10	7	15	13	10	11	12	12	9	16	16	10
17.	11	13	12	10	12	10	14	9	14	10	15	15	14	16	16	15	15	17
18.	13	7	11	13	14	14	13	15	13	15	15	12	16	16	10	17	17	13
19.	11	7	10	13	11	12	10	15	15	15	13	16	11	13	16	15	14	17
20.	13	13	13	14	14	11	14	14	12	7	10	14	9	16	11	15	17	12
21.	10	11	7	10	10	14	8	8	8	10	15	16	13	13	11	16	15	10
22.	13	13	10	13	14	13	11	15	15	15	9	16	16	16	10	14	17	10
23.	13	10	13	14	10	14	14	9	15	15	9	12	10	16	7	16	13	12
24.	13	8	10	13	13	13	11	15	11	13	15	16	16	13	8	16	12	17
25.	10	13	13	11	11	14	12	11	13	15	8	12	9	16	3	11	16	16
26.	12	11	13	14	14	14	14	15	13	11	12	13	16	11	9	16	17	15
27.	13	12	11	13	14	13	12	15	15	15	13	14	15	15	5	12	17	17
28.	9	13	12	12	11	14	14	13	9	14	15	15	13	16	12	17	13	15
29.	13	13	11	11	12	13	12	11	15	13	8	12	16	15	8	13	11	14
30.	13	13	8	14	14	14	7	15	10	15	14	16	15	16	6	15	17	13
31.	12	175	13	11	11	29	11	15	14	8	6	10	6	10	8	16	11	13
32.	9	132	12	13	3	9	7	13	12	18	7	11	12	11	4	11	16	10
33.	13	146	10	13	10	39	6	11	10	28	8	16	9	9	10	14	14	12
34.	12	137	13	14	4	59	8	15	15	38	7	15	4	12	7	17	17	7
35.	13	150	13	12	9	99	6	7	13	48	11	13	8	8	5	15	14	6
36.	8	103	9	7	5	19	8	13	13	58	6	16	5	4	6	17	17	3
37.	13	109	12	6	12	69	5	15	10	68	8	13	7	2	7	16	15	7
38.	13	217	11	5	7	89	9	14	15	78	5	12	13	13	5	15	12	8
39.	8	210	9	8	6	49	5	13	14	88	5	15	10	1	8	15	12	6
40.	13	201	13	4	8	79	9	15	14	98	2	16	11	5	3	17	17	5
41.	12	24	6	6	101	124	4	137	14	7	13	157	102	63	99	6	9	11
42.	6	7	7	8	106	243	7	674	7	17	23	156	104	42	199	4	8	8
43.	9	60	9	12	132	537	3	561	10	27	33	163	106	95	299	10	10	10
44.	3	50	1	2	151	896	7	738	8	37	43	162	101	84	399	3	17	8
45.	8	80	8	4	112	658	11	273	13	47	53	185	103	76	499	2	12	10
46.	11	90	5	10	157	365	24	476	5	57	63	184	144	58	70	5	3	6
47.	5	70	3	9	134	432	365	943	11	67	73	126	166	37	90	1	14	1
48.	7	70	4	5	24	789	263	365	9	77	83	125	182	19	80	7	6	4
49.	4	90	10	3	7	973	473	897	6	87	93	174	125	21	50	9	11	9
50.	10	80	2	7	365	411	492	245	12	97	103	173	157	65	90	8	7	11

Math Speed Tests – Book 1 © World Teachers Press® – www.worldteacherspress.com

Test	44	46	47	48	49	51	52	53	54	56	57	58	59
1.	15	8	6	18	13	15	19	19	19	12	20	20	17
2.	16	18	16	14	18	19	13	12	13	20	13	16	18
3.	17	18	18	11	13	18	15	11	19	12	15	20	20
4.	13	17	15	18	13	19	15	19	13	20	14	14	19
5.	14	15	18	18	15	19	19	13	19	13	13	20	15
6.	17	18	15	8	18	12	17	19	14	20	20	20	20
7.	16	18	18	18	14	19	19	12	19	14	15	13	20
8.	17	15	13	11	18	18	15	14	11	15	10	17	15
9.	17	14	12	11	14	19	13	19	19	20	20	20	20
10.	17	18	13	18	13	18	19	11	19	16	14	19	16
11.	13	14	16	18	13	17	13	14	15	14	16	13	20
12.	14	8	12	8	18	19	18	19	15	20	17	13	15
13.	17	18	15	18	15	19	19	11	19	16	20	14	20
14.	17	14	14	12	18	19	13	14	19	18	13	20	15
15.	17	12	18	9	13	18	19	19	11	20	20	14	20
16.	17	14	18	18	15	12	19	11	19	15	13	10	15
17.	15	13	17	18	15	19	17	15	11	20	14	20	20
18.	11	18	16	18	18	16	12	19	19	17	20	10	13
19.	17	12	17	18	18	17	19	11	13	6	14	20	20
20.	17	17	14	10	16	18	9	15	13	20	12	15	18
21.	15	16	8	18	17	19	19	11	19	17	10	15	14
22.	15	18	14	10	18	29	16	19	19	18	20	10	20
23.	13	15	16	12	14	39	19	19	12	16	15	20	13
24.	14	14	12	18	16	49	19	18	19	20	18	16	19
25.	17	18	14	13	18	59	17	19	12	19	16	20	20
26.	17	12	10	15	7	69	14	19	13	3	15	11	14
27.	17	18	13	18	9	79	19	11	19	13	7	20	20
28.	13	8	11	18	8	89	14	12	13	6	17	11	16
29.	17	13	12	13	9	99	19	13	19	16	18	19	14
30.	13	11	18	7	12	109	13	19	19	1	14	20	20
31.	9	14	3	15	9	13	$1.25	12	7	11	16	9	2
32.	19	16	13	5	0	3	$1.60	15	14	9	19	12	12
33.	29	15	23	12	8	9	$1.70	19	11	19	11	15	6
34.	39	18	33	2	7	10	$1.30	12	6	5	12	7	16
35.	49	8	43	13	3	16	$1.55	15	13	15	10	14	1
36.	59	13	53	3	8	6	$2.70	19	12	7	13	16	11
37.	69	18	63	16	6	15	$3.05	11	7	17	9	16	5
38.	79	14	73	6	6	5	$2.05	19	12	8	6	14	15
39.	89	13	83	9	5	18	$3.20	12	8	18	4	10	7
40.	99	11	93	8	7	8	$3.50	19	13	7	8	13	17
41.	$1.53	$1.53	11	1 m 25 cm	123 cm	16	80	643	8	6	56	33	110
42.	$1.45	$1.77	7	1 m 86 cm	138 cm	26	30	374	6	7	67	43	50
43.	$1.64	$1.92	14	1 m 21 cm	170 cm	36	70	898	9	7	33	84	140
44.	$1.10	$1.85	1	1 m 53 cm	108 cm	46	20	585	14	6	63	62	140
45.	$1.89	$1.42	6	1 m 97 cm	191 cm	56	60	459	9	6	49	96	140
46.	$2.46	$1.63	9	1 m 3 cm	201 cm	66	40	961	15	10	79	86	120
47.	$3.51	$1.55	14	1 m 72 cm	217 cm	76	90	216	10	8	78	62	110
48.	$4.78	$1.01	5	2 m 4 cm	345 cm	86	10	561	10	4	76	77	130
49.	$5.28	$1.20	8	2 m 89 cm	453 cm	96	50	127	11	8	47	46	130
50.	$8.46	$2.96	12	5 m 78 cm	681 cm	106	0	732	16	11	51	88	100

Super Speed Test – 9

#		#	
1.	9	51.	7
2.	5	52.	9
3.	2	53.	8
4.	8	54.	8
5.	9	55.	6
6.	7	56.	6
7.	3	57.	8
8.	6	58.	7
9.	8	59.	9
10.	7	60.	6
11.	4	61.	6
12.	8	62.	9
13.	1	63.	9
14.	3	64.	3
15.	5	65.	8
16.	5	66.	9
17.	9	67.	5
18.	9	68.	5
19.	4	69.	5
20.	3	70.	7
21.	3	71.	8
22.	7	72.	7
23.	8	73.	7
24.	5	74.	1
25.	9	75.	8
26.	9	76.	7
27.	7	77.	7
28.	5	78.	7
29.	6	79.	8
30.	5	80.	4
31.	5	81.	4
32.	8	82.	8
33.	6	83.	8
34.	8	84.	9
35.	7	85.	8
36.	7	86.	8
37.	7	87.	9
38.	7	88.	6
39.	6	89.	9
40.	9	90.	4
41.	3	91.	4
42.	9	92.	9
43.	9	93.	9
44.	2	94.	6
45.	4	95.	9
46.	8	96.	9
47.	9	97.	6
48.	8	98.	4
49.	2	99.	6
50.	2	100.	10

Super Speed Test – 10

#		#	
1.	6	51.	10
2.	6	52.	10
3.	8	53.	8
4.	9	54.	8
5.	3	55.	8
6.	10	56.	8
7.	6	57.	7
8.	6	58.	10
9.	7	59.	10
10.	6	60.	9
11.	7	61.	8
12.	10	62.	6
13.	8	63.	2
14.	4	64.	5
15.	8	65.	7
16.	8	66.	3
17.	8	67.	5
18.	5	68.	3
19.	5	69.	5
20.	8	70.	2
21.	8	71.	3
22.	5	72.	4
23.	10	73.	6
24.	5	74.	3
25.	8	75.	2
26.	5	76.	1
27.	5	77.	4
28.	8	78.	2
29.	10	79.	0
30.	10	80.	7
31.	8	81.	9
32.	10	82.	4
33.	10	83.	9
34.	9	84.	8
35.	10	85.	8
36.	10	86.	0
37.	8	87.	1
38.	9	88.	7
39.	10	89.	10
40.	9	90.	2
41.	10	91.	1
42.	3	92.	0
43.	9	93.	3
44.	6	94.	0
45.	9	95.	5
46.	6	96.	1
47.	10	97.	6
48.	7	98.	4
49.	9	99.	6
50.	7	100.	2

Super Speed Test – 15

#		#	
1.	10	51.	7
2.	11	52.	9
3.	10	53.	11
4.	11	54.	11
5.	10	55.	7
6.	11	56.	7
7.	10	57.	10
8.	11	58.	10
9.	10	59.	9
10.	11	60.	8
11.	10	61.	10
12.	11	62.	11
13.	9	63.	4
14.	10	64.	5
15.	10	65.	11
16.	11	66.	11
17.	10	67.	11
18.	9	68.	6
19.	10	69.	6
20.	10	70.	11
21.	11	71.	7
22.	9	72.	11
23.	11	73.	9
24.	9	74.	8
25.	11	75.	11
26.	9	76.	11
27.	11	77.	7
28.	9	78.	8
29.	11	79.	11
30.	9	80.	11
31.	11	81.	10
32.	10	82.	6
33.	10	83.	11
34.	11	84.	9
35.	10	85.	5
36.	11	86.	11
37.	11	87.	8
38.	11	88.	11
39.	11	89.	7
40.	10	90.	10
41.	10	91.	24
42.	10	92.	35
43.	11	93.	47
44.	11	94.	28
45.	11	95.	38
46.	10	96.	26
47.	11	97.	41
48.	10	98.	39
49.	10	99.	27
50.	11	100.	32

Super Speed Test – 20

#		#	
1.	9	51.	12
2.	9	52.	9
3.	12	53.	11
4.	12	54.	10
5.	9	55.	10
6.	12	56.	10
7.	9	57.	12
8.	9	58.	12
9.	9	59.	10
10.	12	60.	10
11.	9	61.	10
12.	12	62.	11
13.	12	63.	12
14.	9	64.	12
15.	9	65.	10
16.	9	66.	10
17.	12	67.	11
18.	12	68.	10
19.	9	69.	11
20.	9	70.	11
21.	9	71.	10
22.	12	72.	11
23.	12	73.	11
24.	9	74.	10
25.	12	75.	10
26.	12	76.	11
27.	9	77.	11
28.	10	78.	11
29.	10	79.	11
30.	10	80.	12
31.	10	81.	11
32.	10	82.	12
33.	12	83.	12
34.	12	84.	11
35.	9	85.	12
36.	9	86.	11
37.	10	87.	11
38.	10	88.	11
39.	12	89.	11
40.	12	90.	12
41.	10	91.	12
42.	9	92.	11
43.	10	93.	7
44.	12	94.	11
45.	12	95.	11
46.	9	96.	11
47.	12	97.	7
48.	12	98.	11
49.	10	99.	11
50.	12	100.	11

Super Speed Test – 25

#		#	
1.	13	51.	13
2.	13	52.	10
3.	9	53.	12
4.	9	54.	13
5.	13	55.	12
6.	13	56.	13
7.	8	57.	12
8.	13	58.	12
9.	13	59.	13
10.	8	60.	13
11.	13	61.	11
12.	7	62.	12
13.	13	63.	13
14.	13	64.	12
15.	13	65.	13
16.	7	66.	12
17.	13	67.	13
18.	6	68.	13
19.	13	69.	12
20.	13	70.	12
21.	6	71.	13
22.	13	72.	13
23.	5	73.	13
24.	13	74.	12
25.	13	75.	13
26.	5	76.	13
27.	10	77.	13
28.	10	78.	12
29.	10	79.	11
30.	10	80.	10
31.	13	81.	13
32.	10	82.	9
33.	10	83.	11
34.	9	84.	11
35.	13	85.	10
36.	13	86.	13
37.	10	87.	11
38.	13	88.	11
39.	10	89.	12
40.	13	90.	13
41.	10	91.	11
42.	13	92.	13
43.	13	93.	11
44.	10	94.	13
45.	13	95.	10
46.	13	96.	13
47.	13	97.	10
48.	12	98.	13
49.	12	99.	10
50.	10	100.	11

Super Speed Test – 30

#		#	
1.	14	51.	14
2.	7	52.	13
3.	14	53.	14
4.	7	54.	13
5.	7	55.	14
6.	14	56.	13
7.	7	57.	13
8.	14	58.	14
9.	14	59.	14
10.	14	60.	13
11.	7	61.	12
12.	14	62.	14
13.	14	63.	14
14.	14	64.	11
15.	7	65.	12
16.	14	66.	12
17.	14	67.	14
18.	7	68.	2
19.	14	69.	14
20.	14	70.	12
21.	14	71.	12
22.	8	72.	14
23.	14	73.	11
24.	8	74.	14
25.	14	75.	14
26.	14	76.	11
27.	8	77.	11
28.	14	78.	12
29.	8	79.	12
30.	8	80.	11
31.	14	81.	11
32.	13	82.	14
33.	13	83.	14
34.	14	84.	11
35.	14	85.	12
36.	13	86.	12
37.	13	87.	11
38.	14	88.	11
39.	14	89.	12
40.	14	90.	12
41.	13	91.	20
42.	13	92.	20
43.	14	93.	40
44.	13	94.	40
45.	14	95.	60
46.	13	96.	33
47.	14	97.	55
48.	13	98.	46
49.	14	99.	25
50.	14	100.	68

Super Speed Test – 35

#		#	
1.	14	51.	9
2.	15	52.	19
3.	12	53.	29
4.	15	54.	39
5.	12	55.	49
6.	15	56.	59
7.	13	57.	69
8.	12	58.	79
9.	15	59.	89
10.	15	60.	99
11.	13	61.	13
12.	15	62.	11
13.	12	63.	15
14.	14	64.	10
15.	15	65.	14
16.	12	66.	15
17.	13	67.	15
18.	15	68.	14
19.	11	69.	11
20.	13	70.	10
21.	12	71.	15
22.	22	72.	13
23.	32	73.	14
24.	42	74.	13
25.	52	75.	10
26.	62	76.	15
27.	72	77.	11
28.	82	78.	14
29.	92	79.	11
30.	102	80.	15
31.	15	81.	15
32.	14	82.	25
33.	13	83.	35
34.	15	84.	45
35.	11	85.	55
36.	14	86.	65
37.	12	87.	75
38.	15	88.	85
39.	12	89.	95
40.	14	90.	105
41.	13	91.	40
42.	13	92.	50
43.	15	93.	60
44.	12	94.	70
45.	15	95.	90
46.	11	96.	75
47.	15	97.	52
48.	12	98.	37
49.	12	99.	78
50.	14	100.	49

Super Speed Test – 40

#		#	
1.	15	51.	8
2.	13	52.	18
3.	15	53.	28
4.	15	54.	38
5.	11	55.	48
6.	16	56.	58
7.	15	57.	68
8.	14	58.	78
9.	16	59.	88
10.	15	60.	98
11.	14	61.	13
12.	14	62.	11
13.	16	63.	16
14.	12	64.	15
15.	16	65.	10
16.	16	66.	7
17.	15	67.	16
18.	13	68.	10
19.	16	69.	15
20.	9	70.	14
21.	2	71.	13
22.	12	72.	16
23.	22	73.	16
24.	32	74.	12
25.	42	75.	8
26.	52	76.	16
27.	62	77.	13
28.	72	78.	8
29.	82	79.	9
30.	92	80.	16
31.	10	81.	70
32.	15	82.	90
33.	13	83.	50
34.	16	84.	100
35.	11	85.	60
36.	16	86.	90
37.	11	87.	90
38.	16	88.	40
39.	14	89.	80
40.	16	90.	80
41.	14	91.	6
42.	16	92.	10
43.	12	93.	14
44.	16	94.	2
45.	12	95.	8
46.	16	96.	13
47.	10	97.	3
48.	15	98.	11
49.	9	99.	7
50.	16	100.	15

	Super Speed Test – 45			Super Speed Test – 50			Super Speed Test – 55			Super Speed Test – 60	
1.	10	51.	50	1.	11	51.	70	1.	12	51.	18	1.	10	51.	5
2.	12	52.	70	2.	18	52.	100	2.	13	52.	11	2.	20	52.	9
3.	15	53.	90	3.	15	53.	90	3.	15	53.	17	3.	11	53.	6
4.	11	54.	50	4.	18	54.	80	4.	19	54.	9	4.	20	54.	0
5.	13	55.	80	5.	9	55.	60	5.	18	55.	13	5.	12	55.	1
6.	11	56.	70	6.	13	56.	100	6.	15	56.	19	6.	11	56.	4
7.	12	57.	90	7.	14	57.	80	7.	13	57.	13	7.	10	57.	8
8.	10	58.	100	8.	14	58.	70	8.	13	58.	7	8.	10	58.	3
9.	13	59.	80	9.	11	59.	80	9.	12	59.	12	9.	20	59.	2
10.	12	60.	80	10.	18	60.	100	10.	19	60.	18	10.	11	60.	7
11.	13	61.	12	11.	12	61.	2	11.	16	61.	13	11.	20	61.	13
12.	10	62.	16	12.	18	62.	12	12.	12	62.	7	12.	11	62.	14
13.	11	63.	0	13.	13	63.	7	13.	19	63.	6	13.	10	63.	14
14.	11	64.	7	14.	18	64.	7	14.	10	64.	6	14.	20	64.	20
15.	12	65.	7	15.	16	65.	8	15.	12	65.	7	15.	10	65.	13
16.	11	66.	13	16.	7	66.	10	16.	17	66.	8	16.	11	66.	20
17.	12	67.	2	17.	12	67.	0	17.	17	67.	12	17.	12	67.	13
18.	10	68.	14	18.	18	68.	8	18.	10	68.	1	18.	20	68.	14
19.	14	69.	8	19.	10	69.	9	19.	17	69.	5	19.	10	69.	15
20.	13	70.	8	20.	18	70.	11	20.	10	70.	2	20.	20	70.	20
21.	7	71.	17	21.	12	71.	1	21.	19	71.	11	21.	19	71.	15
22.	3	72.	5	22.	18	72.	17	22.	15	72.	6	22.	13	72.	20
23.	7	73.	9	23.	18	73.	7	23.	10	73.	4	23.	17	73.	15
24.	4	74.	15	24.	10	74.	5	24.	11	74.	15	24.	14	74.	14
25.	11	75.	2	25.	18	75.	15	25.	11	75.	10	25.	12	75.	16
26.	10	76.	7	26.	16	76.	6	26.	19	76.	5	26.	18	76.	20
27.	8	77.	10	27.	12	77.	16	27.	7	77.	7	27.	15	77.	13
28.	0	78.	2	28.	18	78.	4	28.	9	78.	9	28.	11	78.	20
29.	6	79.	6	29.	18	79.	13	29.	15	79.	8	29.	10	79.	16
30.	7	80.	11	30.	10	80.	3	30.	15	80.	3	30.	16	80.	13
31.	17	81.	99	31.	11	81.	33	31.	12	81.	7	31.	12	81.	8
32.	17	82.	89	32.	15	82.	66	32.	19	82.	7	32.	20	82.	8
33.	16	83.	79	33.	15	83.	99	33.	9	83.	4	33.	10	83.	7
34.	17	84.	69	34.	8	84.	44	34.	11	84.	3	34.	12	84.	8
35.	17	85.	59	35.	18	85.	88	35.	19	85.	14	35.	20	85.	8
36.	16	86.	49	36.	11	86.	22	36.	11	86.	6	36.	11	86.	8
37.	5	87.	39	37.	16	87.	55	37.	18	87.	5	37.	13	87.	6
38.	15	88.	29	38.	10	88.	101	38.	14	88.	8	38.	20	88.	8
39.	16	89.	19	39.	14	89.	77	39.	19	89.	6	39.	12	89.	8
40.	16	90.	9	40.	18	90.	135 cm	40.	7	90.	7	40.	20	90.	13
41.	17	91.	17	41.	16	91.	113 cm	41.	11	91.	132	41.	13	91.	99
42.	15	92.	27	42.	18	92.	172 cm	42.	11	92.	245	42.	12	92.	199
43.	17	93.	37	43.	10	93.	122 cm	43.	19	93.	728	43.	11	93.	299
44.	17	94.	47	44.	18	94.	164 cm	44.	14	94.	967	44.	20	94.	399
45.	9	95.	57	45.	14	95.	184 cm	45.	18	95.	563	45.	20	95.	499
46.	16	96.	67	46.	14	96.	197 cm	46.	16	96.	845	46.	12	96.	599
47.	17	97.	77	47.	13	97.	179 cm	47.	11	97.	452	47.	20	97.	699
48.	17	98.	87	48.	13	98.	153 cm	48.	14	98.	699	48.	10	98.	799
49.	9	99.	97	49.	18	99.	103 cm	49.	14	99.	856	49.	11	99.	899
50.	17	100.	107	50.	7	100.	146 cm	50.	19	100.	389	50.	20	100.	999

Math Speed Tests – Book 1

Super Speed Test – 61

#		#	
1.	14	51.	14
2.	18	52.	7
3.	6	53.	13
4.	8	54.	19
5.	12	55.	18
6.	20	56.	15
7.	2	57.	17
8.	0	58.	8
9.	10	59.	20
10.	4	60.	12
11.	16	61.	16
12.	8	62.	6
13.	9	63.	10
14.	11	64.	10
15.	9	65.	20
16.	16	66.	14
17.	20	67.	18
18.	18	68.	14
19.	18	69.	20
20.	13	70.	10
21.	13	71.	20
22.	14	72.	4
23.	15	73.	20
24.	20	74.	8
25.	20	75.	18
26.	7	76.	24
27.	4	77.	23
28.	2	78.	13
29.	3	79.	42
30.	14	80.	20
31.	6	81.	24
32.	9	82.	28
33.	0	83.	16
34.	7	84.	11
35.	12	85.	11
36.	10	86.	11
37.	9	87.	11
38.	8	88.	19
39.	7	89.	21
40.	6	90.	23
41.	5	91.	24
42.	4	92.	15
43.	3	93.	9
44.	2	94.	16
45.	1	95.	90
46.	20	96.	65
47.	20	97.	60
48.	20	98.	40
49.	0	99.	40
50.	19	100.	36

Assignment 9 – Multiplication 1

Sample Page from World Teachers Press' *Math Homework Assignments* Grade 2

1. (a) Circle two sets of two.

(b) Circle four sets of two.

(c) Circle five sets of two.

2. How many sets of two? _____ How many altogether? _____

How many sets of four? _____ How many altogether? _____

How many sets of three? _____ How many altogether? _____

3. Draw four sets of five pencils.

4. (a) One bicycle has two wheels.

How many wheels do five bicycles have? _____ × _____ = _____

(b) One car has four wheels.

How many wheels do four cars have? _____ × _____ = _____

 Math Speed Tests – Book 1   © World Teachers Press® – www.worldteacherspress.com

Assignment 11 – Division

1. (a) Share 8 equally among four people.

How many for each person? _____

(b) Share 10 equally among five children.

How many for each child? _____

(c) Share 15 equally among three children.

How many for each child? _____

(d) Share 20 equally among four people.

How many for each person? _____

2. (a) Draw 9 bananas. How many groups of 3 can you make? _____

How many in each group? _____ 9 divided by _____ = _____

(b) Draw 16 stars. How many groups of 4 can you make? _____

How many in each group? _____ 16 divided by _____ = _____

Assignment 24 – Time 1

Sample Page from World Teachers Press' *Math Homework Assignments* Grade 3

January

S	M	T	W	T	F	S
1	2	3	4	5	6	7
8	9	10	11	12	13	14
15	16	17	18	19	20	21
22	23	24	25	26	27	28
29	30	31				

February

S	M	T	W	T	F	S
			1	2	3	4
5	6	7	8	9	10	11
12	13	14	15	16	17	18
19	20	21	22	23	24	25
26	27	28				

March

S	M	T	W	T	F	S
			1	2	3	4
5	6	7	8	9	10	11
12	13	14	15	16	17	18
19	20	21	22	23	24	25
26	27	28	29	30	31	

April

S	M	T	W	T	F	S
30						1
2	3	4	5	6	7	8
9	10	11	12	13	14	15
16	17	18	19	20	21	22
23	24	25	26	27	28	29

May

S	M	T	W	T	F	S
	1	2	3	4	5	6
7	8	9	10	11	12	13
14	15	16	17	18	19	20
21	22	23	24	25	26	27
28	29	30	31			

June

S	M	T	W	T	F	S
				1	2	3
4	5	6	7	8	9	10
11	12	13	14	15	16	17
18	19	20	21	22	23	24
25	26	27	28	29	30	

July

S	M	T	W	T	F	S
30	31					1
2	3	4	5	6	7	8
9	10	11	12	13	14	15
16	17	18	19	20	21	22
23	24	25	26	27	28	29

August

S	M	T	W	T	F	S
		1	2	3	4	5
6	7	8	9	10	11	12
13	14	15	16	17	18	19
20	21	22	23	24	25	26
27	28	29	30	31		

September

S	M	T	W	T	F	S
					1	2
3	4	5	6	7	8	9
10	11	12	13	14	15	16
17	18	19	20	21	22	23
24	25	26	27	28	29	30

October

S	M	T	W	T	F	S
1	2	3	4	5	6	7
8	9	10	11	12	13	14
15	16	17	18	19	20	21
22	23	24	25	26	27	28
29	30	31				

November

S	M	T	W	T	F	S
			1	2	3	4
5	6	7	8	9	10	11
12	13	14	15	16	17	18
19	20	21	22	23	24	25
26	27	28	29	30		

December

S	M	T	W	T	F	S
31					1	2
3	4	5	6	7	8	9
10	11	12	13	14	15	16
17	18	19	20	21	22	23
24	25	26	27	28	29	30

1. How many months are there in one year? _____

2. How many days are in March? _____ February? _____ May? _____

3. How many days in one year? _____

4. Circle your birthday in purple.

5. Color the following days in red and write the day it falls on.

Christmas _____ Thanksgiving _____

New Year's Day _____ Valentine's _____

6. How many Thursdays are there in October? _____

7. What is the date on the third Friday of May? _____

8. What is the date of the first Wednesday in June? _____

9. What date is the second Monday of the third month? _____

 Math Speed Tests – Book 1   © World Teachers Press® – www.worldteacherspress.com

NOTES

NOTES

NOTES

NOTES

Math Speed Tests – Book 1 © World Teachers Press® – www.worldteacherspress.com

NOTES

NOTES

Math Speed Tests – Book 1   © World Teachers Press® – www.worldteacherspress.com

NOTES

NOTES